The *"PRACTICAL GREEN"*
Retirement Abode

ISBN: 979-8-218-64558-8

Cover photo by DJ

other photo's by author unless noted for nephew DJ

DEDICATED TO:

Nance (editor & big Pooter Mom)
Kristina (now big Pooter)
Grant (new little Pooter)
Zach (little Pooter Dad)

Because . . . they had to listen to this technical construction stuff all those years!

and to the Falklands . . . because of their foster start gift to me

by : Art Smith, April 2025

CONTENTS

CHAPTER 1 – INTRODUCTION TO "PRACTICAL"

LET's GET REALISTIC . . . FAST !

But, absolutely first:

If you prefer many of the <u>cosmetically cute</u> home design features seen on the typical "Reality" Home TV shows, you should save your time and money at not proceeding with this booklet.

If you are past middle age, and desire to build a home (not a trivial process at any age !!) specifically for better retirement living, we will here, in much technical detail, offer a solid plan to assist one to build a <u>safe</u>, <u>comfortable</u>, <u>low-energy</u> use, and <u>low-maintenance</u>, version. And . . . in the ballpark cost range of typical homes, while very much suited for that phase of life. (& likely a good "starter" home for many!)

Many of these design factors are covered in more technical detail in the author's two earlier works :
(<u>**Building Today's Green Home,**</u> *by Art Smith, 2009, &* **Simple S.I.P. Homes**, *by Art Smith, 2020).*

For brevity in this intended short booklet a coded/colored scheme will refer to book, Chapter, page, Drawing figure, etc. in sections covering this technical background. *(Example is: > BTGH, C2, P19 < for* first book, **> SSIP, C3, P24 <** for second book.)

Let's begin with defining what "Practical" really means here.

Our sharp focus here is on just several fundamental points: Overwhelmingly oriented to common sense <u>utility</u> factors (not "cute" or just cosmetic features only)

- *"Comfortable" and "Safe" living environment for elderly years*
- *Living on <u>one floor level</u>*
- *Realistic size, <u>not "tiny"</u>, yet not oversized*
- *Low energy use (& add some Passive Solar heat winter gain = adds to "safety" element)*
- *Low maintenance, particularly to exterior issues*
- *Stronger structure than typical framing, particularly roof & walls (again, safety!)*

But before we lay out the specifics of <u>**what will be in**</u> our new chosen floor plan, let's call out what won't

be . . . so this is our *"DON'T"* list:

*** DON'T LIST ***

1- No stair/steps within or entryways to home
2- No 2X4 <u>exterior</u> walls
3- No "ventilated" pitched roof/flat ceiling designs (see > SSIP, C3, P63, Fig. 3.17<)
4- No overly steep roof pitches, like 8, 10, & 12/12 (see > SSIP, C3, P63, Fig. 3.17<)
5- No "GABLE-ITUS" (excessive number of gables, or double rakes) . . . very specifically:
    Dual roof gables close together forming "roof funnel" to under-length rain gutter
6- No "DORMER-ITUS" (NO dormers at all ! . . . unless actually provides rear-of-house daylight)
7- No wood-based exterior siding (period)
8- No wood <u>exterior</u> doors (cute rots!)
9- No asphalt shingles (go metal, fastened, or standing seam $$)
10- No fiberglass batt or other batt type insulations
11- No "tray ceilings"
12- No decorative "returns" on gable end bottom corners
13- No full glass or sliding glass doors
14- No dual or "patio" doors
15- No overly tall (54" maximum), or narrow, or multiple-gang windows
16- No double-hung windows
17- No muntins, mullins, decorative grilles, etc. in windows
18- No overly decorative trim (like "crown")
19- No <u>ducted</u> , central HVAC system

20- No gas powered heating, water, or oven (Unless extreme north climate dictates for heating)
21- No overly large kitchen <u>Island</u> bar counter (like Australia size?)
22- No sink in bar Island counter (clutters area & disrupt's Island's primary function)
23- No overly large/fancy bathtubs like "soaking" or "Sauna" (rarely use, plumbers now removing !)
24- No fancy kitchen exhaust vents with exposed tall vertical vent (limits top cabinet space)
25- No potentially large growing shrubs near house (smaller, planters/pots, seasonal perinials, better)
26- <u>No wearing of jeans with pre-ripped holes near the knees !</u>
(partially kidding here, because #26 & previous 25 list frequently share a common trait: "**FAD's**")

If the reader is irritated by some/most of this **<u>Don't List</u>**, I have to surmise you did not heed my first page opening warning. As a sanity check on the impact of these <u>extra features</u> in your home, I suggest that one should do a quick cost analysis of the above "fancy" set. Do this at two levels: about one half of the list and then the total list. (Please utilize a "real-world" experienced construction assistant for this.)

The above cost analysis will likely shock you if not even at the half level, but definitely will at the full-list total. The reality is that many of these features are currently in USA residential construction. And really disturbing is that the inclusion of these 'fancy' features <u>almost always knocks out</u> (for budget reasons) the quality points we aim to include in a more realistic "Retirement" home! In summary, this yields:

"<u>What is typically Built</u>"

Then add to the "Fancy Features" cost just completed to the other looming monster in the room:

Physical home size !

- *Most mature Americans know the growth of the home size inflation in their lifetime*
- *One source noted: 50 year <u>average</u> of all the US home sizes is about 1900 sf in 3 bed, 2 bath layout*
- *Current new homes range in 2200-2400 sf from the early 2000's to now (slight dip, post 2008 crash)*
- *My parents 1959 Alabama ranch was 864sf (24ft x 36 ft footprint)*
- *Even my own modest retirement home at 1536sf is almost 2X of my parents 1959 "ranch" !*
- *So, something smaller than 1900 sf is likely a good <u>starting point of size</u> determination*

Thus, one must add this "larger size" cost figure than needed at retirement time to the budget decision process. Or, the <u>true total cost</u> is both the extra "size" cost penalty added to the "Fancy feature" cost list. Our primary goal is that our final cost of the smaller, higher real quality, retirement home is close to a larger, lower quality, "Typical construction" home. However, even if we do have some net cost increas of the **<i>"practical"</i>** version over the **<i>"typical"</i>** version, this is still a successful strategy!

(Think of also adding in the long-term energy & maintenance issues)

Let's do a quick, but very conservative estimate, of a typical "size penalty" if we use the 1900sf as the top limit and then the extra 300 sf (over a 1600sf house) subset cost. At the minimum, it is $100 per s.f. (likely higher). Just this step results in a base of $30,000 for the size increase, but realistically may be $40K plus. Add the "fancy feature costs" and now we have some real budget dollars to work with to <u>improve quality</u>!

If the reader needs one more example of what "Typical" construction yields the homeowner in real-world situations, please review the reports from the "freak" snowstorm that swept through Texas in February 2021. It shut down power and water for up to a week in some districts. In fact, one elderly couple were found frozen to death in their living room chairs. If your house temperature falls into the 30's on the inside, it should be a warning shot to a mature adult that you have a problem! And even more alarming if you do not have back-up source for heat, water, or electricity. I thus challenge readers to ponder on the concept of spending your entire productive life working earnestly and then have your "retirement" living zone as risky as that. Also ponder on the many weather videos we all see after one of Mother Nature's tornado or hurricane events This has happened multiple times, so it is not freak! Thus, the fancy features and the larger size of "typical built" did not help those people trapped in that situation.

<i>Now let's outline the key technical features for our "practical" floor plan which actually will be revealed in the drawings in the Chapter 2.</i>

KEY STRUCTURAL ELEMENTS:

1 - WALLS:

- Mainly S.I.P. (Structural Insulated Panels), 6-1/2" thick, R22 rating (usually EPS)
- Non - SIP exterior walls = 2x6 & POST framed, typically on south wall with large windows
- Likely be pre-framed in shop (use inclement weather), trailered to shop for wall-lift day
- Anchor bolts (1/2") holes pre-drilled in sill plates

2 - FOUNDATION:

- Site choice and lot grading design to strive to only need slab/footing foundation !!
- Insulate under slab (R10) and slab edges as local code allows:
  > Southern 7 states not allow EPS foam under slab because of termite migration
  > Some other foam-ish solutions exist? Like Corning FoamGlas® (even R4-R6 is helpful)
  > With or w/o "under-slab", 1-1/2" (R6) x 4" FoamGlas® bonded to slab edge perimeter is key
- Foundation straps in footings tie to truss posts @ 64" centers/house corners (Simpson LSTH8)
- "Hold-Down" brackets like the Simpson HD3B have hold forces greater than 1 ton each, using the 1/2" Hilti bolt as in Figure 3.3 "custom" bracket example (thus, about 2 tons per post)
- A combination of corner straps, post straps, and even the extra post brackets can net 28 hold-down points with at least 30 tons of house hold-down force (High wind regions)
- Straps can use Simpson SDS 1-1/2" screws (100# ea.?), or TimberLok 2-1/2" screws (200# + ?)
- Then add in the hold-down of the Hilti bolts into the slab for the PT sill plates (50 bolts, 50 tons ?)
- Don't use the typical builder "mud-sill" thin metal, nail down, straps - just minimal !

3 - ROOF STRUCTURE:

- Timber (not 2x4 - based) trusses, glu-lam Engineered wood, ¼" steel plates, & 5/8" bolts
- 2x8 Pine T&G roof decking over trusses & gable walls (with 64" spacing 3x= 16 ft lengths, = interleave row pattern of 64", 128", & 196")
- 9-1/4" thick EPS foam panels (R37) on T&G with top ½" CDX sheaving (panel screws into T&G) nets R39 total insulated roof rating
- Nets much stronger than typical southern USA 20# s.f. roof loading !!
- See >SSIP, C3, P63, FIG3.17< for details of structural "sandwich" ,modest vaulted roof

4 - EXTERIOR:

- First choice is brick . . . or :
- Siding to be fiber-cement based (like HARDIE ®), preferably wood textured panel (4'x8' or 9') size with board & batten patten trim (1x3 or 1x4, about 16-24" spacing)
- Any exterior trim is fiber cement based (like HARDIE ® 1x3 or 1x4's)
- Could be lap siding, or even limited "shingle" on just top of gable ends (pricing = 3-4x)
- Or even low-height, wainscot brick to just under window ledges (mix with siding above)

5 - WINDOWS:

- Prefer aluminum clad/wood or newer fiberglass (brands like Jeld-Wen $$, Pella $$, or Marvin $$$)
- Some other quality "Regional" window manufacturers (like Lincoln or Sun) available ?
- Strongly suggest upgrade to triple pane, EnergyStar rated glass (over normal double pane)
- No Solar Heat Gain limiting coating needed, usually South USA required (proper window overhangs = sun shading in summer,& allows maximum sun "in" for winter days)

6 - WALL INSULATION:

- Spray foam, low density, 5-1/2" thick, R22 (like SIP's value) in the south framed 2x6 walls
- Also spray foam similar in the above top plate zones between the tall truss heel ends
- Note: if in far north, consider 8" wall SIP's & 11-1/4" (R45) roof foam (or polyurethane)

7 - ROOFING:

- Standing Seam metal (preferred if have budget for)
- Or: fastener-attached metal (use ZAC fasteners, better grade than typical "builder grade")
- And key: Ice/Water membrane over *entire roof sheathing*

8 - HVAC SYSTEM:

- House heat/cool J-Manual rating about 1-1/2 tons range (for southeast USA, higher more north)
- Ductless Mini-split system, likely mix of single compressor units, or maybe one dual ??
- Standard 9000BTU "Indoor unit" in Great Room & "Study" > SSIP, C3, P56, FIG3.16<
- Guest bedroom and maybe the Master Bedroom could use the smaller 6000BTU, if available
- Typical freon line/electrical bundle from outdoor compressor to indoor units try to maximize the 12"x12" *UTILITY CHASE* in the north wall. >SSIP, C3, P56, FIG3.16<
- Mini-splits not in bath's, just small resistant heat strips, with smart Temperature control
- Bath has EnergyStar rated exhaust fans (Panasonic FV-0511VQ1)
- Energy Recovery Ventilators (ERV), suggest two smaller units, each end of house (for re-cycling fresh air into the home with minimal energy loss – Panasonic FV-06EV1)

9 - PASSIVE SOLAR GAIN NOTES:

- If owner's building lot enables mainly south facing windows ("South" noted on drawing):
- Then, with proper roof shading overhang length for south windows! > BTGH, C9, P99 <
- The 159 s.f. of 11 south windows shown here will generate about 238K BTU total on "average" winter day = about 9900 BTU/hr-rate (Appendix 1, Mazria's "Passive Solar" book, page 402)
- Equals: ¾ ton of heating per hour = roughly ½ of the houses heat load on "average clear day"
- Means even with power outage & w/o wood stove . . . home temperature is in "safe" range

10 - OVERALL ENERGY USE GOAL:

- Generally follow *"EnergyStar"* guidelines as minimum
- But . . . some recent requirements are "too academic" and not as practical:
  - > Overly requiring Heat-Pump style hot water heaters (costly, not as reliable, and not usually have the *lifetime tank* of the Marathon version)
  - > Re-circulating plumbing for distant bath from hot water tank (expensive, less reliable, and energy saving costs not realistic)
- "Certification" fees by expert rater agents have grown rapidly
- If one really wants an *official* "GREEN " certification, can justify costs within budget, then go for it !

But first, a rough summary from a recent Georgia Power note is a very useful reference:
>**The average total-electric Georgia home uses just over 2000 KWH per month**
>**Thus the average power bill is over $300 per month**

Now let's compare how most of these concepts performed in the author's three prior homes in over four decades.

AUTHOR's THREE-HOME, 4 PLUS-DECADE's EXPERIENCE SUMMARY

(NOTE: All were "total electric", heat pump heating/cooling, with some Passive Solar heat gain)

1 - FIRST ENERGY EFFICIENT HOME APPROACH: *(from 1981 to 2001)*

- Location: *just northeast of Atlanta, Georgia*
- Author's contribution: *Designed home, some carpentry, had General Contractor (GC) for most construction*
- Floor area: *1920 sf in 3 bed, 2 bath plus extra den, footprint about 26ft x 46ft*
- Configuration: *Most rooms on main level, with Master Bed/Bath/Study up on partial, house-rear, 2nd floor*
- Roof style: *offset clerestory, 4/12 south, 2nd floor (rear) also 4/12 (Gap for south upper floor windows)*
- Ceiling structure: *4x8 exposed beams with thick T-111 Plywood, R19 foam panels, top sheathing*
- "Bermed/Basement" West & North walls *(10" poured reinforced concrete, w/ R10 external insulation)*
- Non-bermed wall framing = *2x6, with thin foam sheets & R19 fiberglass batts*
- Originally cedar shake shingles *(never do again!)* replaced with 40 year asphalt shingles *(not also)*
- Exterior siding : *Cedar horizontal boards, channel rustic pattern, cedar trim boards (So-so lifespan)*
- Windows were *early double pane, but aluminum frame (pre-EnergyStar)*
- Approximate "Energy Code" at build: *Walls = R11, Roof = R19*
- HVAC: *Central ducted heat pump, about 2 tons size, SEER (efficiency) at time = 10*
- Average power usage per month (total electric): *about 1100 KWH*

2 - MID-LIFE HOME VERSION: *(1998 weekend cabin, full-time residence from 2001 to 2015)*

- Location: *in the north Georgia mountains, at 2200 ft elevation*
- Author's contribution: *Designed home, built steel roof trusses, some carpentry, had General Contractor (GC)*
- Floor area: *main floor was 1250 sf in 2 bed, 2 bath plus small den, footprint 24ft x 52ft*
- Configuration: *All major rooms on main level: Master bed/master bath/2nd bed/2nd bath/small Study*
- With steep mountain lot, had only south-half basement, 170 *finished* sf there, 450 sf more not finished
- Roof style: *offset clerestory, 4/12 south, north was 6/12 pitch, Gap for few south small upper vent windows*
- Ceiling structure: *6x6 exposed pine beams, @ 24", 1x6 T&G deck, R30 foam panels, top sheathing*
- Basement concrete walls, *10" poured, reinforced with R10 external insulation*
- Wall framing = *2x6, with thin foam sheets & R19 fiberglass batts*
- Roof shingles were *concrete tiles (reasonably durable, but can crack if walked on or by tree limb fall)*
- Brick, *with some veneer (flat) stone sections*
- Windows were *double pane, but aluminum clad frame (was close to now, EnergyStar rating)*
- Approximate "Energy Code" at build: *Walls = R11, Roof = R30 (soon go to R39, for Appalachian range)*
- HVAC: *Central ducted heat pump, about 1-1/2 tons size, SEER (efficiency) at time = 13*
- Average power usage per month (total electric): *about 1000 KWH*

3 - PLANNED-FOR-RETIREMENT HOME: *(early 2016 on)*

- Location: *north Georgia, just south of Appalachian mountain ridge*
- Author's contribution: *Designed home, built Timber-Trusses, main carpenter, was GC, some sub-out work*
- Floor area: *main is 1536sf in 2 bed, 2 bath, footprint 24ft x 64ft (Master Bed & Great Room , like book's)*
- Configuration: *Most rooms on main level, "Hobby" loft & small office (spare bed) in partial, open loft (+360sf)*
- Roof style: *full length "Wedge" 4/12 Timber Trusses, 64" spacing, taller south wall nets small loft zone*
- Ceiling structure: *2x8 EWP, T&G decking, 10+" EPS foam panels, top sheathing, total roof rating = R43*
- Not level enough lot, still some partial basement & *insulated/sealed* short crawl space for balance
- Basement concrete walls, *10" poured, reinforced, R10 external insulation (R10, house slab floor, elevated)*
- Passive Solar windows mix is *about 175 sf on South, 15 sf on North (2 small), none East & West*
- Wall framing = *2x6, with open cell spray foam (R22), glulam posts, corners, etc, with foundation straps*
- Roof is *attached metal, upgraded gauge and finish, with ZAC commercial grade screws*
- Exterior: *Brick, with cement-based board trim, stainless steel siding nails*
- Windows: *Triple pane, aluminum clad over wood frame (EnergyStar rating)*
- Approximate "Energy Code" at build: *Walls = R13, Roof = R39*
- HVAC: *Ductless, mini-split, heat pump, triple-indoor, single compressor, about 2 tons size, SEER = 20*
- Average power usage per month (total electric): *For entire 107 months, 710 KWH = $96/month*
- Rough estimate portion-per-month: *water heat = $15-$20 (thus, gas not save much), heat/cool = $40-$80*

And folks . . . inside temp's will never get near 32 degrees, nor 40's, nor low 50's !

With our rules established, let's view our suggested floor plan utilizing these concepts next :

CHAPTER 2 - FLOOR PLAN INTRODUCTION

By applying the technical concepts in the prior section and then factoring in what a reasonable size home for retirement style living will be, we present the floor plan on the next page with a <u>brief overview</u> here of the general "design intent" per room (more details "by ZONE" comments, as implemented, in Chapter 6):

MASTER BEDROOM:

- *Nice, but realistic size, Queen size bed fits well, bookcases, dressers, & nice walk flow zones*
- *Large south window triple set = good daylighting*

MASTER BATH:

- *Nice size, double sink, but <u>only</u> shower here, <u>some handicap spacing</u> ease*
- *Nice hamper & linen with rear door ("magic") to adjacent closet laundry zone = ease of use*

MASTER CLOSET:

- *Good clothes hanging sides, but not intended for mid-life career wardrobe needs*
- *Washer/Dryer and rear hamper access simplifies laundry tasks*
- *Corner counter space adds utility for laundry handling*
- *Shelf room above hangers, but limit to 80-84" height, for "reachable" storage*

KITCHEN:

- *Comfortable size, but not huge "full growing family" size*
- *Realistic bar counter island, but allow for more handicap spacing, if needed*
- *Small walk-in pantry closet near refrigerator (with potential expansion space)*

DINING:

- *Spacious (maybe long 7' table ?), even length for temporary-added "Holiday" 2nd table*
- *Nice window arrangement & wall space for adjacent Hutch/Dish storage unit*

LIVING:

- *Good cozy, not huge, seating zone with main sofa & two side chair zones*
- *Good mix of TV viewing spacing, wood stove, and still nice window set view out*

GUEST BEDROOM:

- *Reduced size for "short-term" guests, not intended as Handicap-Access*
- *Could still have Queen size bed (with one aisle) & some realistic closet space*

GUEST BATH:

- *Medium size, regular tub & shower (or +), not handicap access (need one tub in house !)*
- *Vanity & linen cabinets may be "custom" size shape to optimize spacing*

STUDY:

- *"Multi-purpose" room, 2 distinct office nooks, hobby table, bookshelves & file storages*
- *Central Futon/pull-out bed for <u>extra</u>, but <u>limited</u>, guest bed (beyond "Guest" bedroom's)*

So, let's check out our proposed Floor Plan on the next page . . .   *See Figure 2.1 next page >>*

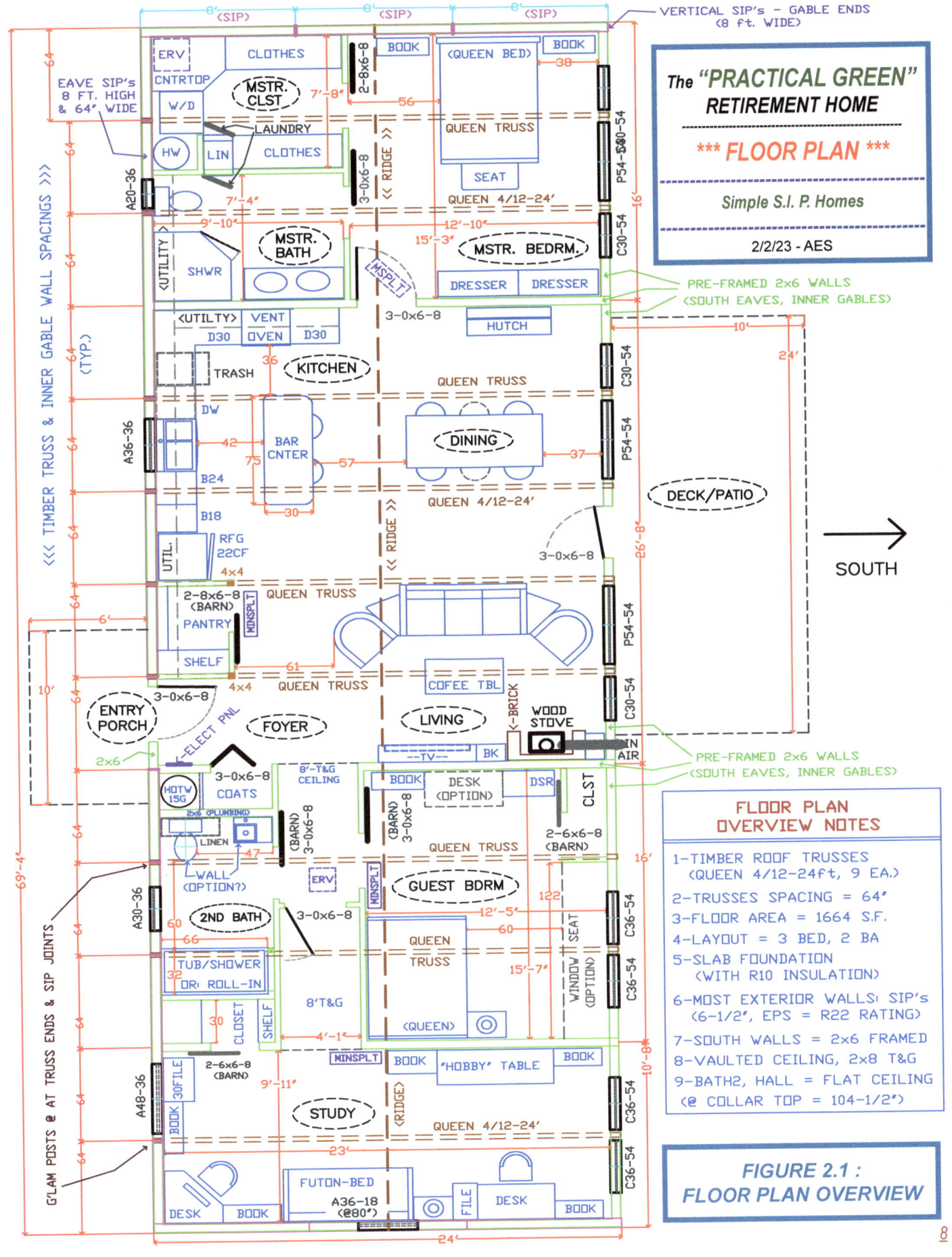

The "PRACTICAL GREEN" RETIREMENT HOME

*** FLOOR PLAN ***

Simple S.I. P. Homes

2/2/23 - AES

FLOOR PLAN OVERVIEW NOTES

1-TIMBER ROOF TRUSSES
(QUEEN 4/12-24ft, 9 EA.)

2-TRUSSES SPACING = 64'

3-FLOOR AREA = 1664 S.F.

4-LAYOUT = 3 BED, 2 BA

5-SLAB FOUNDATION
(WITH R10 INSULATION)

6-MOST EXTERIOR WALLS: SIP's
(6-1/2", EPS = R22 RATING)

7-SOUTH WALLS = 2x6 FRAMED

8-VAULTED CEILING, 2x8 T&G

9-BATH2, HALL = FLAT CEILING
(@ COLLAR TOP = 104-1/2")

**FIGURE 2.1 :
FLOOR PLAN OVERVIEW**

SOUTH

8

ELEVATION DRAWINGS:

Now with our concept floor plan revealed, let's check how our "simplified ranch" exterior appears at the street view, or in "Elevation" drawings. But, even before viewing these two elevations of our proposed "realistic, later-in-life", floor plan with our focus shifted to the _interior being "more comfortable"_ than the exterior being "_cute_" merits a sneak peak on this style interior ceiling.

Thus, our stronger, Timber-Truss based, Great Room's vaulted interior, T&G structural 2x wood-decked, modest 4/12 pitch ceiling (ridge beam 4 ft above eave) looks like:

SO . . . HERE ARE "THE RULES" FOR THE TWO ELEVATION DRAWINGS SHOWN NEXT:

- _We only show the South (Figure 2.2) & West (Figure 2.3) elevations in basic form (two other sides will look very similar)_
- _Porch roof overhangs, deck railings, similar trim details, left for owner's taste to refine_
- _South exterior is brick "wainscot" to under window ledge height (other 3 sides, mainly brick)_
- _Non-brick surfaces utilize cement based (Like Hardie®) panels (4'x8' sheets, etc)_
- _Board/batten trim over the panel sections (1x3 verticals at 16" centers)_
- _Window and other trim typically 1x4 Hardie®) boards_
- _Most of the West (& East) gable end is brick to about the top wall plate line (Eave height)_

General window guide locations per house side:

> _Maximum number of windows on south side (11 in our plan)_
> _Minimum quantity and size on North side (we have 4 smaller ones in this plan)_
> _Note: Just by shifting a window from the south to north = net energy loss_
> _Also, limit windows, if can, on the East & West (particularly west side in southern climates)_
> _High center awning shown in long "Study" aids in some daylighting & venting (none on East)_
> _If property site requires symmetrical flip, means Study go to East, then no window on West, etc._

THE "PRACTICAL GREEN" RETIREMENT HOME

*** SOUTH ELEVATION ***

Simple S.I.P. Homes

2/2/23 - AES

69'-4"

FIGURE 2.2 - SOUTH ELEVATION VIEW

GENERAL COMMENTS ON THE TWO ELEVATION DRAWINGS:

- *The brick surfaces costs are about $8- $12 per sf., more on upper triangle gables (angle cut waste)*
- *HARDIE ® board & batten in the $6-$8 range (symmetrical panels cuts, used on other gable)*
- *The upper eave roof edge trim can be 2 tiered, bottom 1x10, top 1x4 = softens "wide" roof rake*
- *High center awning window for long "Study" daylighting (East has no window)*

WEST & EAST ELEVATION SPECIFIC COMMENTS: *See Figure 2.3 below >>>*

1- The West & East gable ends generally should be brick for low-maintenance, but
2- The upper gable triangle could use some fiber-cement-based "enhancements" :
> Board & Batten, *HARDIE* ® panel behind, 1x3's on 16" centers on top, (as in South elevation)
> *HARDIE* ® fiber-cement shingles (but, about 2-3X cost of board/batten)
3- *HARDIE* ® "shingle" pattern attractive (not shown), but wasted angles costly, more than brick
4- Fiber-cement exteriors still require painting, but their lifetime between re-coats is about 2x of wood surfaces, like 8-12 years vs 4-5. (Also use stainless-steel siding nails vs typical galvanized)
5- Since we now have an impressive <u>interior-vaulted</u>, Timber-Truss ceiling (picture on page 9), with a <u>non-vented</u> roof design, there is *no sensible reason to artificially adding eave height* much past 8 ft eave heights. (details in S.I.P. panel wall related drawings for the actual 8'-3" eave total)

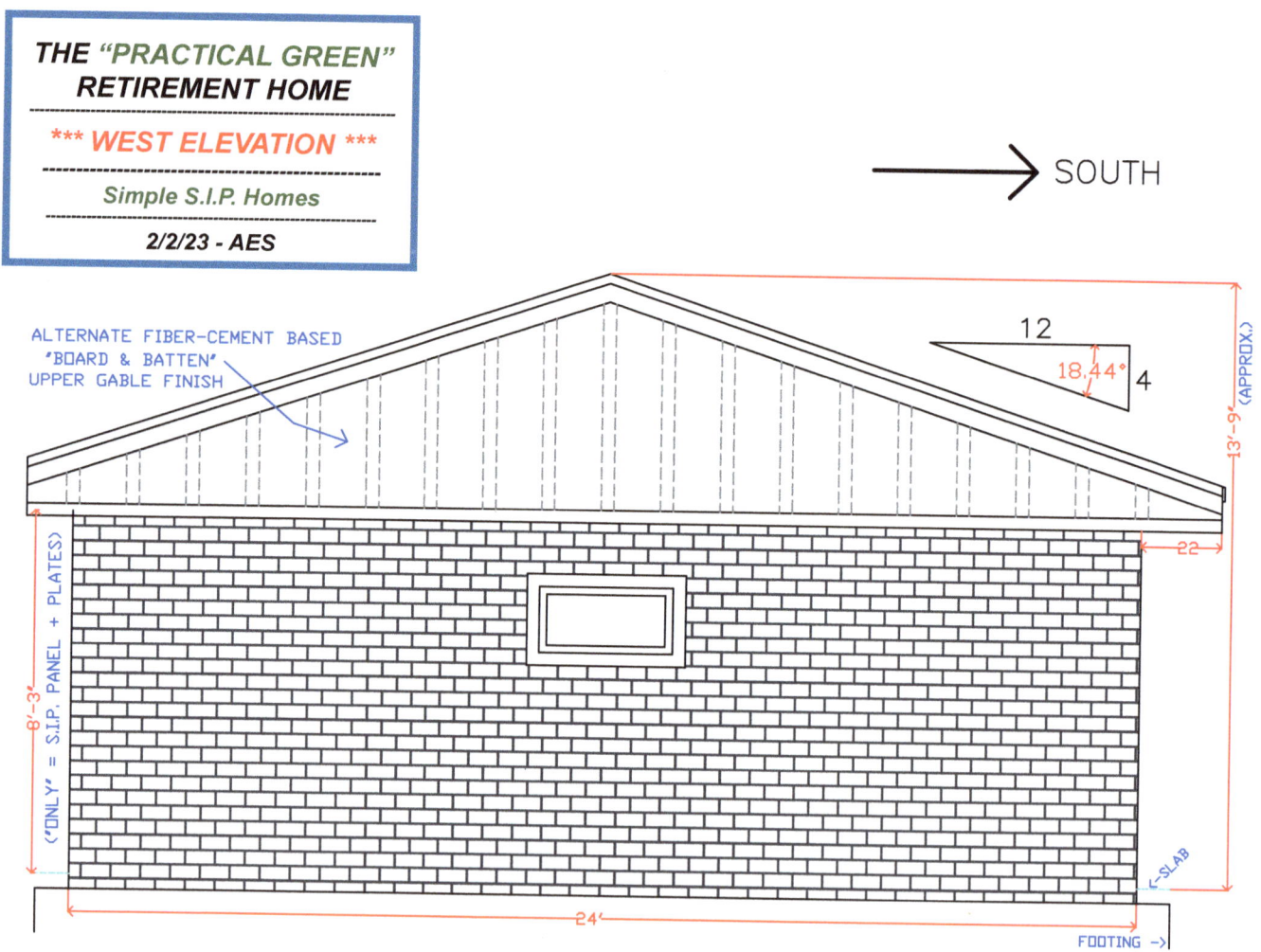

THE *"PRACTICAL GREEN"* RETIREMENT HOME
*** WEST ELEVATION ***
Simple S.I.P. Homes
2/2/23 - AES

SOUTH

ALTERNATE FIBER-CEMENT BASED
"BOARD & BATTEN"
UPPER GABLE FINISH

12
18.44°
4

13'-9" (APPROX.)

22

8'-3" ("ONLY" = S.I.P. PANEL + PLATES)

SLAB

24'

FOOTING →

FIGURE 2.3 - WEST ELEVATION VIEW

CURRENT "DUAL GABLE LOOK" HOMES vs SIMPLER ELEVATIONS: See Figure 2.4 next >>

> *Usually 2 large, likely steep 12/12 pitch "bump-out" gables, about 2/3's of the 60 + ft house width, nets short rain gutters*
> *A lot of rain volume & splash for short gutters (likely water protective membrane only in narrow valley zones)*
> *Even more features added: Dormers (up to 3?), 2nd offset rake edge trim (dashed gray lines below), eave returns, etc*
> *Have actually seen "left-in" 2x4 brace visible in fake window, and three dormers so close, not sure how they were built !*

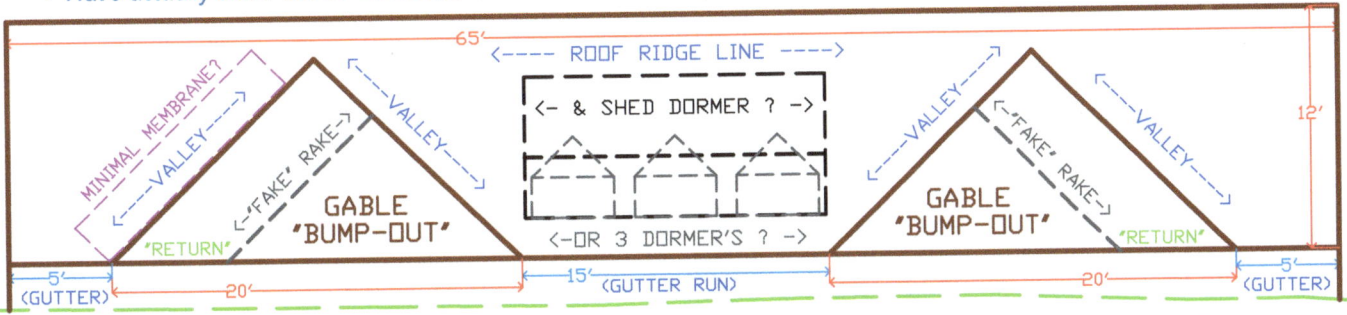

FIGURE 2.4 - POPULAR "DUAL GABLE LOOK" FEATURE EXAMPLES

Our roof build sequence (Nephew DJ's house) near current neighborhood's street views in next photo: (photo by DJ)

TYPICAL CONSTRUCTION   (upper left of photo)
> "vented roof", fiberglass insulation, R19-30 on flat ceiling
> Means "HOT BOX" in ceiling in summer, not work well
> Weak ridge, 2x10 if framed?, none, if pre-fab 2x4 truss ?
> Only 7/16" OSB roof sheath, 1/2" sheetrock in flat ceiling
> Roof water membrane likely only in narrow valley zones
> Frequently, dormer windows are not thru to house (fake)

OUR TIMBER TRUSS/VAULTED ROOF   (foreground)
> Vaulted interior is "conditioned" space (actually used)
> EPS foam panels (2 layers, R30-39) is in roof line
> 1/2" CDX plywood on EPS top layer (w/SIP screws)
> SIP screws "sandwich" CDX, EPS, to thick T&G
> CDX is fully covered with good water membrane
> Dual ridge: top 12" LVL , 6x6 Glu-LAM under (seen)

WHAT ARE THE TYPICAL COSTS FOR THESE COSMETIC FEATURES ?
- *Steep 12/12 main roof is 35% more roof framing/decking material (12/12= +41%, 4/12= +5% roof run)*
- *Each "feature" = maybe $300 to $2K each, if several, total = $6-$12k per house . . . or even more*
- *Some even add taller ceilings (9' or 10', but still flat), just lifted tall house even more (wind resistance?)*

Or: *Shift $ budget for Timber Trusses?, or thicker 2x6 T&G decking?, or standing-seam metal roof ?*

Thus, we should now invest more of our budget for a quality structure than in cosmetic features .

So, let's view even more specific building technologies to improve our future home's integrity :   12

CHAPTER 3 - FOUNDATION PLAN

Since we are committed to a single level floor plan and have chosen a relatively flat build site, a desired "slab foundation" is do-able. I strongly prefer the two 2-step concrete pour where a solid footing base is poured first, and then the slab on top of the footing. (Not a "monolithic" pour)

The next three Figures 3.1, 3.2, & 3.3 demonstrate the hold-down straps at the building corners, strap posts at Glulam SIP posts, and even the "extra" brackets at the larger south window Glulam posts.

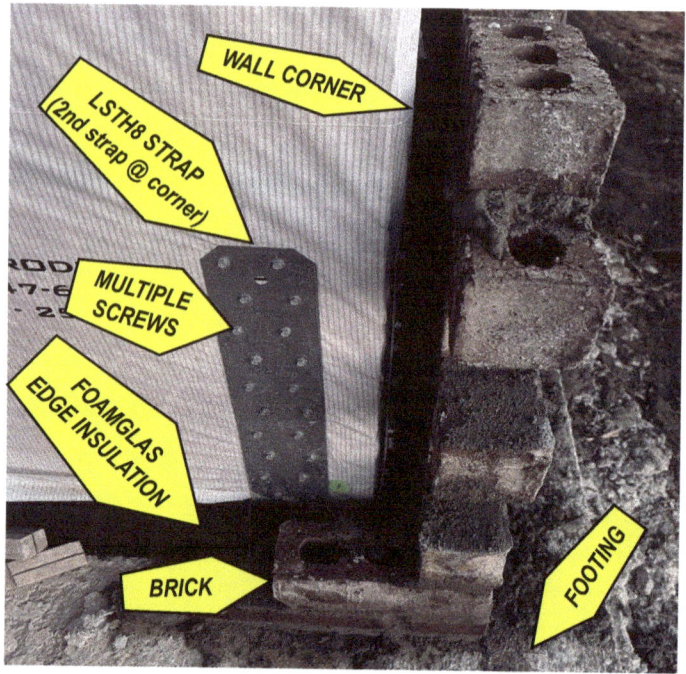

FIGURE 3.1 - TIE-DOWN STRAPS

(photo by DJ)

FIGURE 3.2 - STRAPS @ POUR

(photo by DJ)

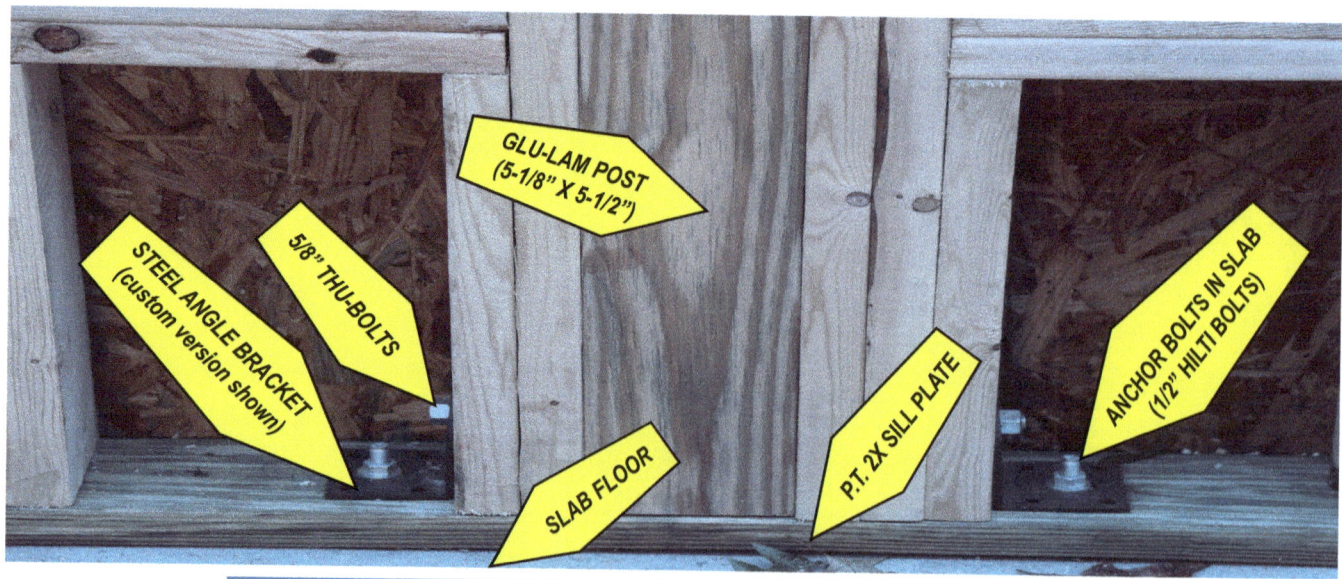

FIGURE 3.3 - POST BRACKETS & SILL PLATE BOLTS

(photo by DJ)

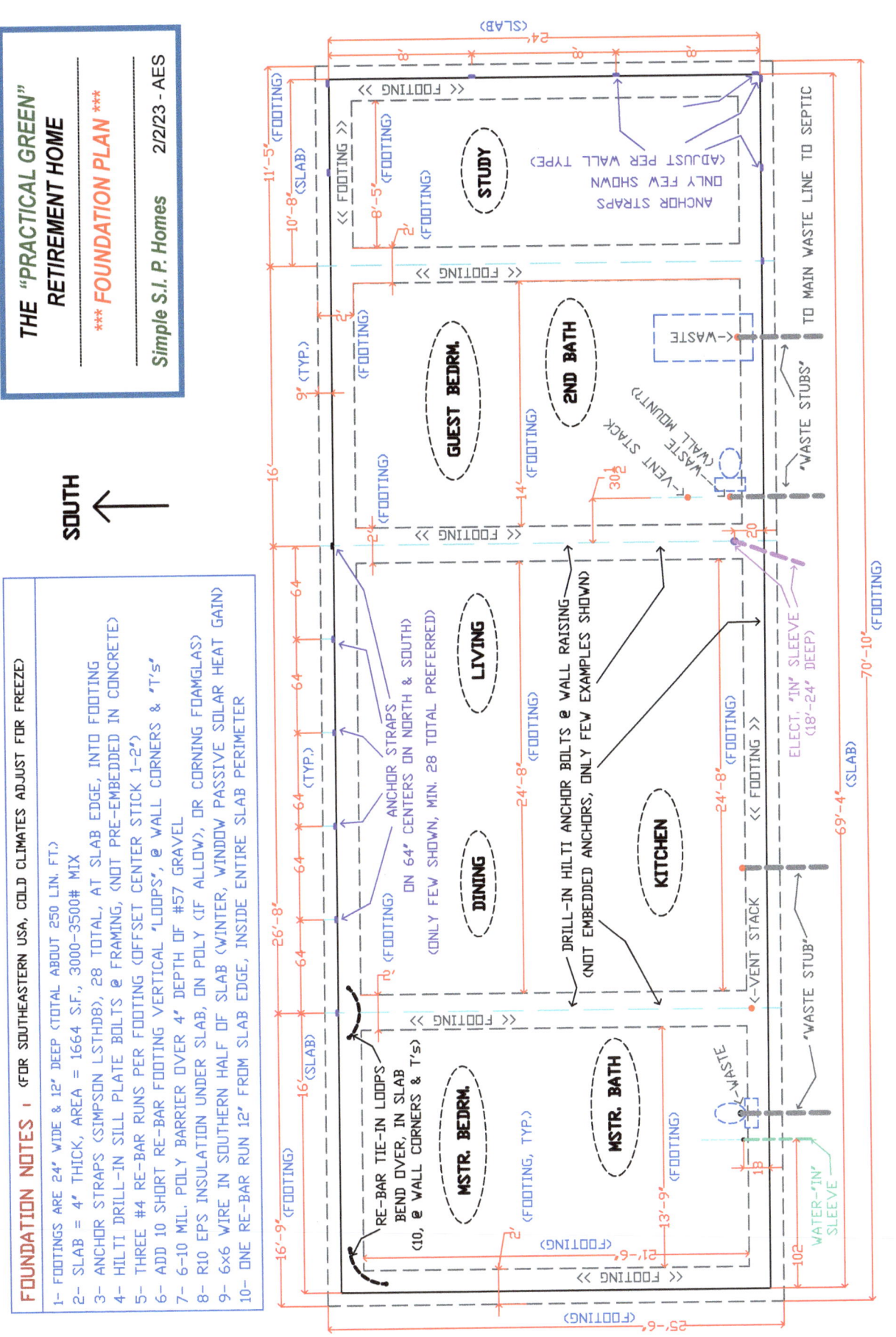

SOUTH ←

FOUNDATION NOTES : (FOR SOUTHEASTERN USA, COLD CLIMATES ADJUST FOR FREEZE)

1– FOOTINGS ARE 24" WIDE & 12" DEEP (TOTAL ABOUT 250 LIN. FT.)

2– SLAB = 4" THICK, AREA = 1664 S.F., 3000-3500# MIX

3– ANCHOR STRAPS (SIMPSON LSTHD8), 28 TOTAL, AT SLAB EDGE, INTO FOOTING

4– HILTI DRILL-IN SILL PLATE BOLTS @ FRAMING, (NOT PRE-EMBEDDED IN CONCRETE)

5– THREE #4 RE-BAR RUNS PER FOOTING (OFFSET CENTER STICK 1-2")

6– ADD 10 SHORT RE-BAR FOOTING VERTICAL "LOOPS", @ WALL CORNERS & "T's"

7– 6-10 MIL. POLY BARRIER OVER 4" DEPTH OF #57 GRAVEL

8– R10 EPS INSULATION UNDER SLAB, ON POLY (IF ALLOW), OR CORNING FOAMGLAS)

9– 6x6 WIRE IN SOUTHERN HALF OF SLAB (WINTER, WINDOW PASSIVE SOLAR HEAT GAIN)

10– ONE RE-BAR RUN 12" FROM SLAB EDGE, INSIDE ENTIRE SLAB PERIMETER

FIGURE 3.4 - FOUNDATION PLAN

14

Labels within plan:

STUDY

ANCHOR STRAPS ONLY FEW SHOWN (ADJUST PER WALL TYPE)

GUEST BEDRM.

2ND BATH

WASTE

TO MAIN WASTE LINE TO SEPTIC

VENT STACK (WALL MOUNT?)

"WASTE STUBS"

LIVING

DINING

KITCHEN

DRILL-IN HILTI ANCHOR BOLTS @ WALL RAISING (NOT EMBEDDED ANCHORS, ONLY FEW EXAMPLES SHOWN)

ANCHOR STRAPS ON 64" CENTERS ON NORTH & SOUTH (ONLY FEW SHOWN, MIN. 28 TOTAL PREFERRED)

VENT STACK

"WASTE STUB"

ELECT, "IN" SLEEVE (18-24" DEEP)

MSTR. BEDRM.

MSTR. BATH

WASTE

RE-BAR TIE-IN LOOPS BEND OVER, IN SLAB (10, @ WALL CORNERS & "T's")

WATER-"IN" SLEEVE

(FOOTING)   (SLAB)

(FOOTING)   (FOOTING)

(FOOTING)   (FOOTING)   (FOOTING)   (FOOTING)   (FOOTING)   (FOOTING)   (FOOTING)

(SLAB)   (SLAB)

(FOOTING)   (FOOTING)

Dimensions:

24' (SLAB)

8'   8'

11'-5"

10'-8" (SLAB)

8'-5"

2'

9' (TYP.)

2'

16'

14'

30Ø

2'

26'-8"

64"   64"   64"   64"   64"   64"   64"   64"

(TYP.)

2'   2'

24'-8"

24'-8"

70'-10"

69'-4" (SLAB)

20Ø

16' (SLAB)

25'-6"

21'-6"

13'-6"

10Ø

1Ø

2'   2'

(FOOTING, TYP.)

16'-9"   16'-9"

CHAPTER 4 - WALL TECHNOLOGY (S.I.P.'s) DETAILS

An overview of the four types of wall S.I.P. (Structural Insulated Panel) employed in this modest home is via example SIP industry required "shop drawings" shown next:

1- STANDARD EAVE (on North wall) :   See Figure 4.1
2- CORNER EAVE (on North wall) :   See Figure 4.2
3- DUAL EAVE (on North wall) :   See Figure 4.3
4- GABLE END VERTICAL SIP's (West & East sides) :   See Figure 4.4

STANDARD EAVE PANEL:

Figure 4.1 next on page 16 >>>

The Standard Eave is based upon the standard 8ft high size, but the width is the 64" spacing of the Timber Trusses and internal gable walls. This 64" pattern simplifies the nailing of 16ft (T&G pine decking board length – three 64" = 16 ft) on the ceiling. This enables the preferred "interleaved" row pattern of the ceiling T&G board length offsets of 64", 128", & 192") Since we also want stronger support point under the Timber Truss ends than just the SIP panel, we insert a Glulam post (actual size is 3-1/8" x 5-1/2"). This post fits in to both ends of adjacent panels into the 1-9/16" foam "relief" cavity shown on the following drawing. Note that this 64" wide panel is reasonably handled by 2 to 3 workers (weight about 150 #) and thus not need a boom truck at this stage of wall erecting. The shown "SHOP DRAWING" example also indicates if this style panel would need a window cutout detail like the north kitchen sink window on the floor plan.

CORNER EAVE PANEL :

Figure 4.2 on page 17 >>>

The CORNER Eave is almost the same as the standard eave except it is 6-1/2" narrower. Since the SIP walls are 6-1/2" thick, one of the two house sides needs to be shorter at the overlap junction due to this thickness. We prefer the end gable SIP's (discussed at end of this section) to be the full 24' building width. Thus, the first corner SIP on this north Eave wall has the 6-1/2" width reduction.

DUAL EAVE PANEL :

Figure 4.3 on page 18 >>>

The Dual Eave version is the standard 8ft height, but the width is now two 64" spacings, bringing the total horizontal length to 128" (about 300#, 3-4 workers can tilt up to maneuver, slide, but not dead lift). Thus extra width can be used when you cross an internal 2x6 gable wall where the SIP Joint posts are not needed. (Like the Master Bath to Kitchen area). The standard 8" long SIP screws just attach to the framed 2x6 gable vertical end plate. The 2nd dual panel Shop Drawing for the Guest bedroom should detail the window opening.

GABLE END VERTICAL SIP's :

Figure 4.4 on page 20 >>>

The two gable ends of the house (East & West) are the only sections we use the longer "vertical" oriented SIP panels that can be factory cut from the 24 ft. long OSB sheets. Each gable end consists of three 8ft wide panels to conveniently net the house depth of 24ft. By using the glulam 3-1/8" x 5-1/2" post scheme here also, but with longer posts, and the tops cut to match the 4/12 roof pitch, we yield a stronger three-panel section that can be lifted in one step on the "boom truck day" (also lift the 9 timber trusses just after the gables). Thus, the pre-assembly of these two gable ends can be completed in the center of the Great Room slab, stacked on each other, and between the likely installed PT sill plates on the north wall. One triple section is assembled first with the only the top side nailing completed. The second panel set is then assembled on top of the first section. Now, the lifting bar is then attached nearer the top (when lifted) of the top gable. Note the temporary four, short, 2x6 inserts in the bottom to support the relieved edges of the two OSB sides when lifting the entire section. The bottom surface nailing is completed after the entire gable section is tilted up to a 90 degree position for the few minutes of nailing needed on this, just hidden side when flat. The first triple-panel section is lifted and installed. Then the second gable section similarly follows.

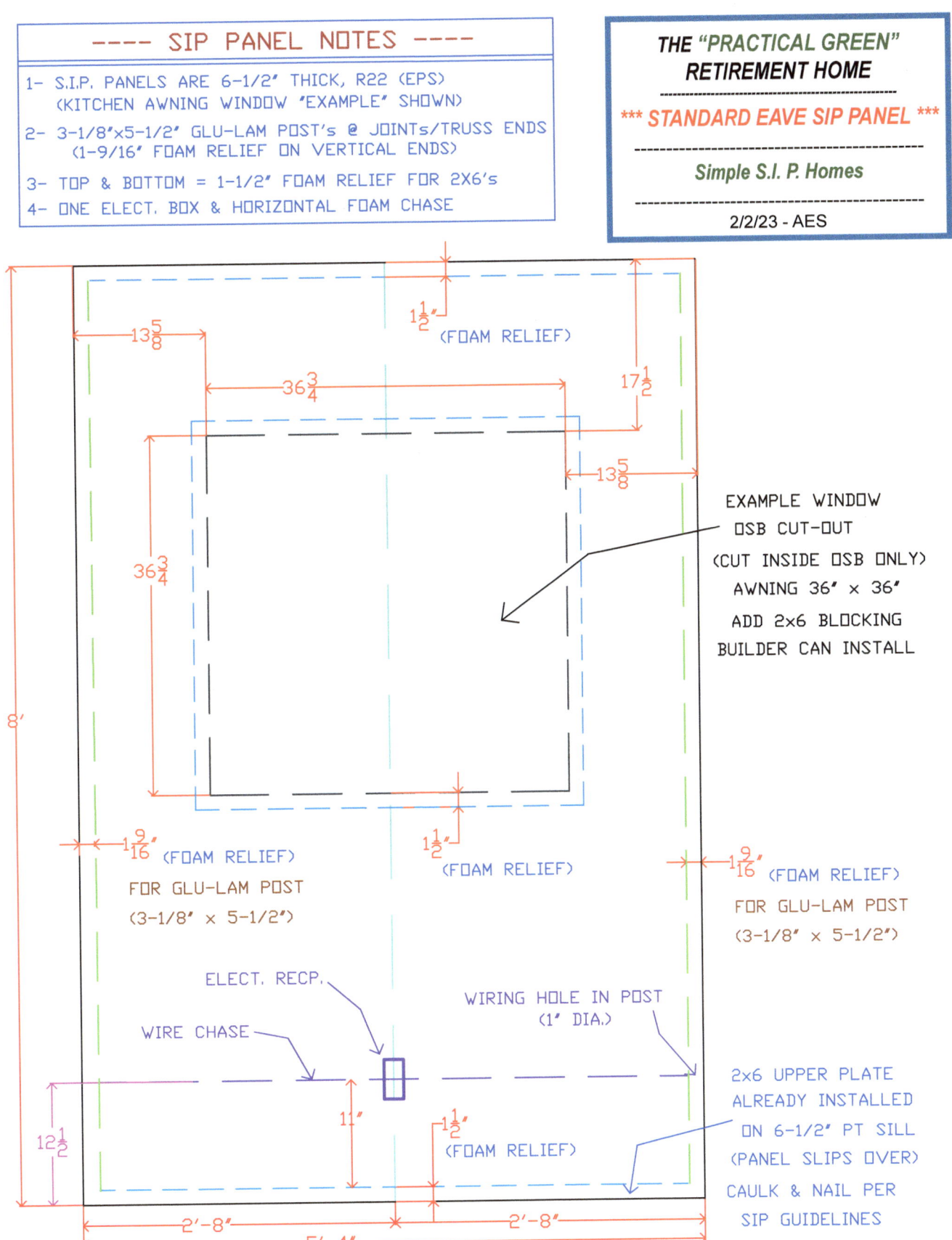

THE "PRACTICAL GREEN"
RETIREMENT HOME

*** STANDARD EAVE SIP PANEL ***

Simple S.I. P. Homes

2/2/23 - AES

$1\frac{1}{2}$" (FOAM RELIEF)

$13\frac{5}{8}$

$36\frac{3}{4}$

$17\frac{1}{2}$

$13\frac{5}{8}$

$36\frac{3}{4}$

EXAMPLE WINDOW
OSB CUT-OUT
(CUT INSIDE OSB ONLY)
AWNING 36" x 36"
ADD 2x6 BLOCKING
BUILDER CAN INSTALL

8'

$1\frac{9}{16}$" (FOAM RELIEF)
FOR GLU-LAM POST
(3-1/8" x 5-1/2")

$1\frac{1}{2}$" (FOAM RELIEF)

$1\frac{9}{16}$" (FOAM RELIEF)
FOR GLU-LAM POST
(3-1/8" x 5-1/2")

ELECT. RECP.

WIRE CHASE

WIRING HOLE IN POST
(1" DIA.)

2x6 UPPER PLATE
ALREADY INSTALLED
ON 6-1/2" PT SILL
(PANEL SLIPS OVER)
CAULK & NAIL PER
SIP GUIDELINES

11"

$1\frac{1}{2}$"
(FOAM RELIEF)

$12\frac{1}{2}$

2'-8"   2'-8"

5'-4"

FIGURE 4.1 - STANDARD "EAVE" SIP PANEL

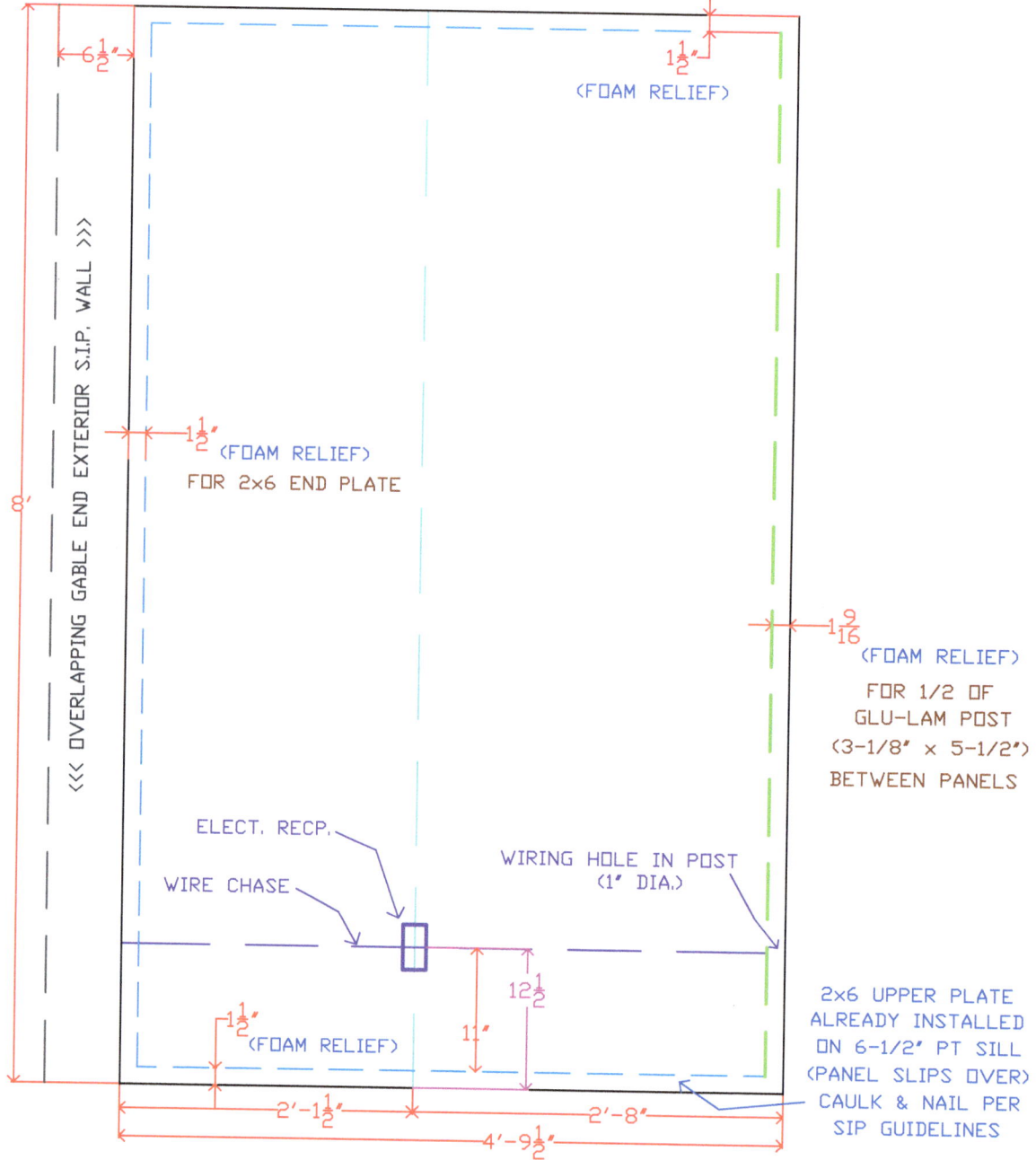

---- SIP PANEL NOTES ----

1- S.I.P. PANELS ARE 6-1/2" THICK, R22 (EPS)

2- 3-1/8"x5-1/2" GLU-LAM POST's @ JOINTs/TRUSS ENDS
   (1-9/16" FOAM RELIEF ON VERTICAL ENDS)

3- TOP, BOTTOM, RIGHT = 1-1/2" FOAM RELIEF FOR 2X6

4- ONE ELECT. BOX & HORIZONTAL WIRE CHASE

5- 1 CORNER FOR N.W. & 1 'MIRROR' VERSION FOR S.E.

THE "PRACTICAL GREEN"
RETIREMENT HOME

*** CORNER EAVE SIP PANEL ***

Simple S.I. P. Homes

2/2/23 - AES

$6\frac{1}{2}$"

$1\frac{1}{2}$"
(FOAM RELIEF)

<<< OVERLAPPING GABLE END EXTERIOR S.I.P. WALL >>>

8'

$1\frac{1}{2}$" (FOAM RELIEF)
FOR 2x6 END PLATE

$1\frac{9}{16}$"
(FOAM RELIEF)
FOR 1/2 OF
GLU-LAM POST
(3-1/8" × 5-1/2")
BETWEEN PANELS

ELECT. RECP.

WIRE CHASE

WIRING HOLE IN POST
(1" DIA.)

$12\frac{1}{2}$

11"

$1\frac{1}{2}$"
(FOAM RELIEF)

2x6 UPPER PLATE
ALREADY INSTALLED
ON 6-1/2" PT SILL
(PANEL SLIPS OVER)
CAULK & NAIL PER
SIP GUIDELINES

2'-1$\frac{1}{2}$"

2'-8"

4'-9$\frac{1}{2}$"

FIGURE 4.2 - "CORNER EAVE" SIP PANEL

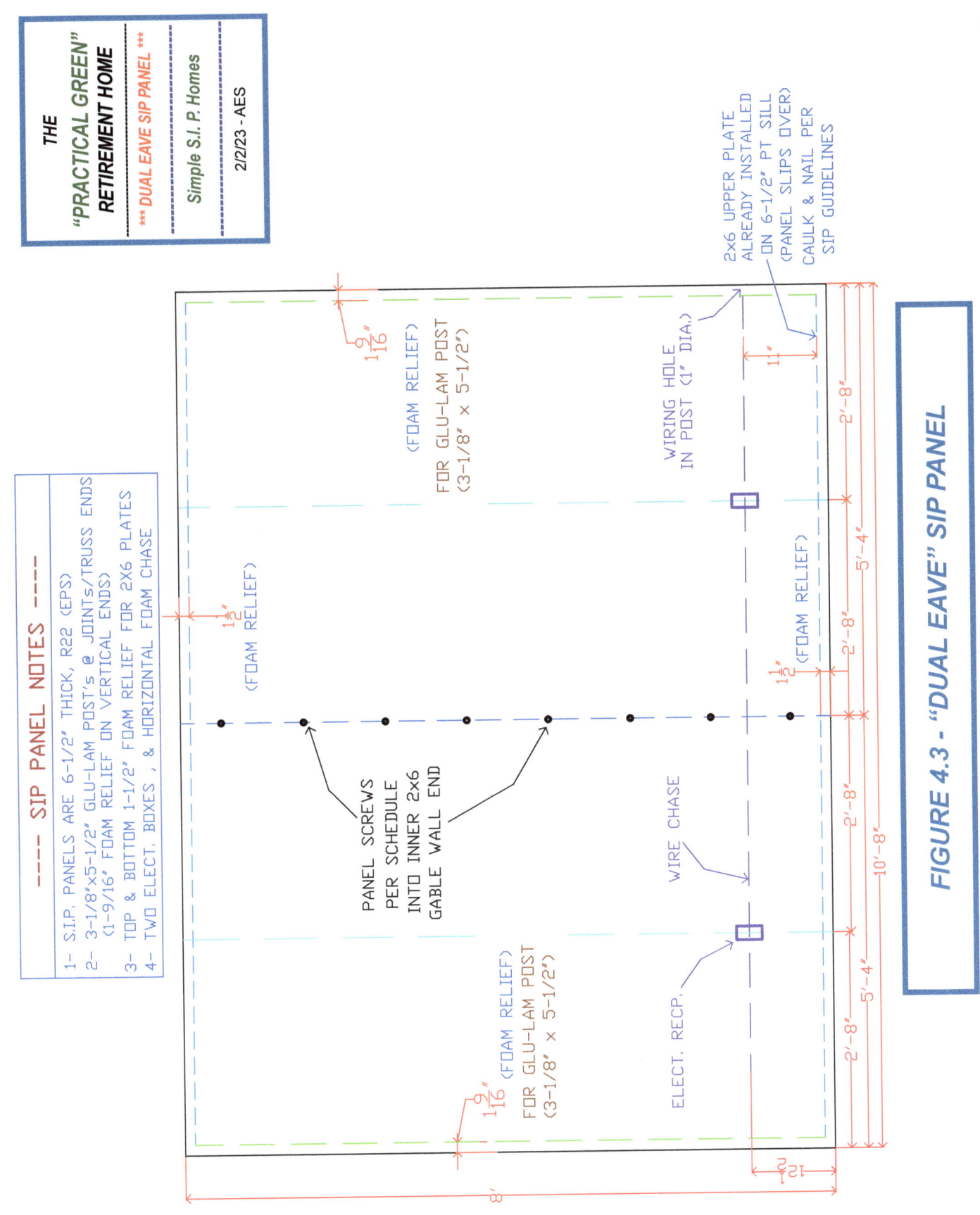

THE
"PRACTICAL GREEN"
RETIREMENT HOME

*** DUAL EAVE SIP PANEL ***

Simple S.I. P. Homes

2/2/23 - AES

---- SIP PANEL NOTES ----

1- S.I.P. PANELS ARE 6-1/2" THICK, R22 (EPS)

2- 3-1/8"x5-1/2" GLU-LAM POST's @ JOINTs/TRUSS ENDS
   (1-9/16" FOAM RELIEF ON VERTICAL ENDS)

3- TOP & BOTTOM 1-1/2" FOAM RELIEF FOR 2x6 PLATES

4- TWO ELECT. BOXES , & HORIZONTAL FOAM CHASE

(FOAM RELIEF)

FOR GLU-LAM POST
(3-1/8" x 5-1/2")

2x6 UPPER PLATE
ALREADY INSTALLED
ON 6-1/2" PT SILL
(PANEL SLIPS OVER)
CAULK & NAIL PER
SIP GUIDELINES

WIRING HOLE
IN POST (1" DIA.)

(FOAM RELIEF)

PANEL SCREWS
PER SCHEDULE
INTO INNER 2x6
GABLE WALL END

WIRE CHASE

ELECT. RECP.

(FOAM RELIEF)

FOR GLU-LAM POST
(3-1/8" x 5-1/2")

FIGURE 4.3 - "DUAL EAVE" SIP PANEL

"CONSTRUCTION AID" TOOL : LIFTING BAR

The fabrication of a custom, safe, (have local PE to verify) structural steel "lifting bar" is a key tool the construction crew <u>must invest in</u>. (see cover picture: **>SSIP<**) One example, with a PE verification locally, may aid the construction crew in building theirs:

See Figure 3.4 for "<u>black</u>" dashed horizontal lines for this bar near 2/3"s of panel height's point

- Can be fully made with one 40 ft. "stick" of C4-5.4# steel structural channel
- Main section uses about 24'-4" for the main beam to span the gable width (with two 9/32" holes in steel at intersection of two glulam posts for 2-1/2" long TimberLOK, by FastenMaster, 5/32" pilot in wood)
- The extra 2" at each end is for welding short C4's, at 90 degrees under the main C4 (welded & spaced at 24ft-1/4" gap - for wall variance tolerance). These short C4's are for bolting to the panel end wall vertical 2x6's (three 2-1/2" long TmberLOK's screws in each 8" C4 vertical stub, in 9/32" dia. holes in steel, 5/32" pilots into wood to be attached to)
- About 14 ft. of remaining C4 section can be "sister" welded along the center rail C4 top, adding stiffness and picking up four more of the TimberLOK screws locations at the two posts intersections.
- Large ½" dia. steel "U" bolts welded appropriately to the main C4 is for lift point cables
- Thus, these about 14 attachment TimberLOK bolt locations (more than 200# pullout each and much higher shear rating) should be in the safe range for lifting the now about 1000# full gable wall end section (and can be installed in, maybe 10-15 minutes, with 2-3 crew and boom truck)

It is important here to advise the construction crew that the synchronization & planning of the smaller SIP north eave wall raising and tied in with the installation of the three pre-framed 2x6 "inner" gables and the five pre-framed 2x6 south eave wall sections in the "second" day before the third "Boom truck day" is key to minimizing labor and bad weather damage on these higher quality modules. (Must cover SIP's for rain, etc.)

This means that the "first day" at site tasks of likely installing the North, East, West 6-1/2" wide (for SIP width) PT sill plate pairs & sill sealer on the slab perimeter coupled with assembling these two large SIP gables on the flat and any unloading/prep work is very key to the timing success. We have, for example, on many projects erected the walls in one day and trusses on part of the second day. My own "WEDGE" retirement home (*See* **>SSIP, C3, P54, FIG3.12 & 3.13<**) with 11 wall sections and 8 wedge timber trusses were <u>all</u> <u>erected</u> in one day with a boom truck and crew of 4. (Actually 3-1/2 . . . I was wearing two knee braces !!)

SILL PLATE BOLTING SCHEME: DRILL-IN-AFTER vs PRE-EMBEDDED IN SLAB

> *We prefer to Hilti bolting to the slab upon raising the walls . . . because :*

> *It is time consuming to fit the sill plate clearance holes over the pre-embedded concrete anchors*

> *And: more flexibility of location changes at a key point in the construction sequence*

> *Example: adding more angle brackets around the south wall window posts after wall erecting*

> *Pre-drilling the 1/2" bolt locations in the wood sill plates in advance, now is a good plan*

Most of the exterior walls will be SIP panels as just discussed. However, some exterior walls, typically with large window openings, are stronger, and better built using a <u>hybrid</u> <u>approach</u> of traditional 2x6 framing, but adding <u>Glulam posts</u> at the key 64" truss end load centers. Note also these larger Glulam posts provide a much stronger attachment mass than even 2x6 size studs for the foundation straps shown in Chapter 2.

Those framing details will be after this Gable End section drawing next on page 20 >>>

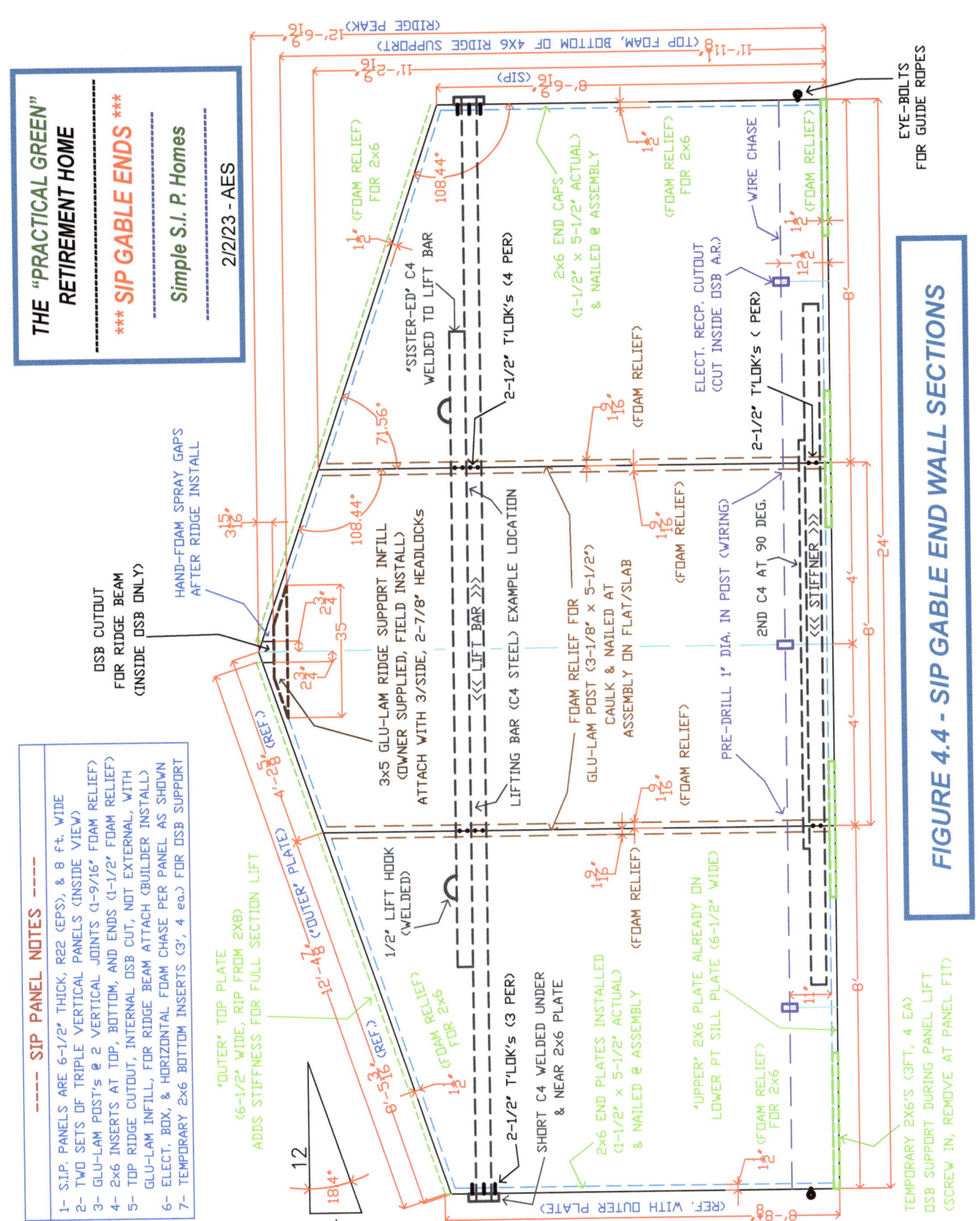

THE "PRACTICAL GREEN" RETIREMENT HOME

*** SIP GABLE ENDS ***

Simple S.I. P. Homes

2/2/23 - AES

---- SIP PANEL NOTES ----

1- S.I.P. PANELS ARE 6-1/2" THICK, R22 (EPS), & 8 ft. WIDE
2- TWO SETS OF TRIPLE VERTICAL PANELS (INSIDE VIEW)
3- GLU-LAM POST's @ 2 VERTICAL JOINTS (1-9/16" FOAM RELIEF)
4- 2x6 INSERTS AT TOP, BOTTOM, AND ENDS (1-1/2" FOAM RELIEF)
5- TOP RIDGE CUTOUT, INTERNAL OSB CUT, NOT EXTERNAL, WITH GLU-LAM INFILL, FOR RIDGE BEAM ATTACH (BUILDER INSTALL)
6- ELECT. BOX, & HORIZONTAL FOAM CHASE PER PANEL AS SHOWN
7- TEMPORARY 2x6 BOTTOM INSERTS (3', 4 ea.) FOR OSB SUPPORT

FIGURE 4.4 - SIP GABLE END WALL SECTIONS

FRAMED *POST* & 2x6 "*SOUTH EAVE*" WALL SECTIONS   See Figures 4.5 - 4.8 following >>

These five south pre-framed 2x6's (16" O.C.) <u>exterior</u> wall sections use the larger "unusual" size glulam 5-1/2" x 5-1/8" posts at the Timber Truss end load points (@ 64" spacing, same source as Truss beams). The 5-1/2" glulam side matches up with the 2x6 wider section as wall depth and the 5-1/8" side with the "unusual" figure used as the width.

This key structurally detail reflects why SIP suppliers should factor in these three related wall strength notes when they offer their product as a solution (generally very good, but not fit well in this special case):

1. *Heavier Timber-Truss <u>end load points</u> need more strength at this 64" spacing location*
2. *Large south windows (for Passive Solar gain) leave little SIP material at truss end points*
3. *We prefer stronger walls (wind?) with stiffer posts that are also aid in <u>foundation straps tie-in</u>*

A quick, rough cost estimate indicates that a typical 8' high SIP panels for each of these five sections will be about $450-$600 each while the framed 2x6's will cost in the $350 to $450 range, including labor (& then add the R22 spray foam charge + $100?). Also, copying the SIP structural feature of the <u>dual OSB</u> walls (about $40 per section for adding the "inside" OSB after spray foaming the R22 wall insulation) on these framed sections increases the wall strength on this important South wall with so many window openings.

GENERAL CONSTRUCTION NOTES FOR THE FIVE FRAMED SOUTH MODULES:

- *Best to be pre-built, in advance, in a shop (bad weather work?, even invest in steel table jigs!)*
- *All five can be trailered to site even on a 16 ft, medium rated, deck-over, trailer*
- *Outside OSB sheathed in shop also, but specific windows/doors per room, cut out at site*
- *Window sizes may be <u>slightly tighter</u> (1/2" Vs ¾") <u>R</u>ough <u>O</u>penings for Jeld-Wen clads*
- *Headers to be insulated: either with 2-1/2" thick EPS (R10) foam panels at assembly, <u>or</u> :*
- *Spray foam 2-1/2" gap at south wall insulating: Drill "in" & "out" holes for spray nozzle to fill*
- *Both Great Room (Dining/Living) modules symmetrical, exterior OSB reversed on one at shop*
- *Pre-drill holes in sill plates for ½" Hilti slab anchor bolts (install Hilti's just after raising walls)*
- *Both the window glulam posts and the SIP gap glulams can be accurately pre-cut prior in shop*
- *Example foundation strap Simpson LSTHD8 on each glulam truss posts:* (As in Figures 3.1 thru 3.3)
  - *Only 10 (of 20) TimberLOK screws, 2-1/2" long = 2000lb + uplift resistance (per post)*
  - *up-size holes for TimberLOK's Vs typical nails*
  - *Could even increase # holes used & more TimberLOK's to 20 maximum for more uplift*
  - *Strap actually on <u>outside of outer OSB</u> (Drawing just indicates general location)*
  - *Alternate: Simpson HD3B Hold-Down bracket pairs with ½" or 5/8" bolts @ post bases*
  - *Could use <u>both brackets & straps</u> for extreme hurricane/tornado zones (Thus "scalable")*
  - *The sill bolts with the post brackets alone will net about ½ of sill plate bolts typically needed*
  - *Also could add LSTHD8 straps: three inner gables ends (6) and SIP exterior gable ends (4)*
  - *Just these about 28 straps, provide about 30 tons of "hold-down" force to foundation*
  - *Note also that the about 50 Hilti bolts in the sill plates is more than 50 tons hold-down there*

BOTTOM LINE:

This <u>hybrid</u> wall-with-post-at-64" centers system, is clearly <u>stronger than all-SIP</u> wall with big holes in the SIP material !! . . . for this <u>specific case !</u>

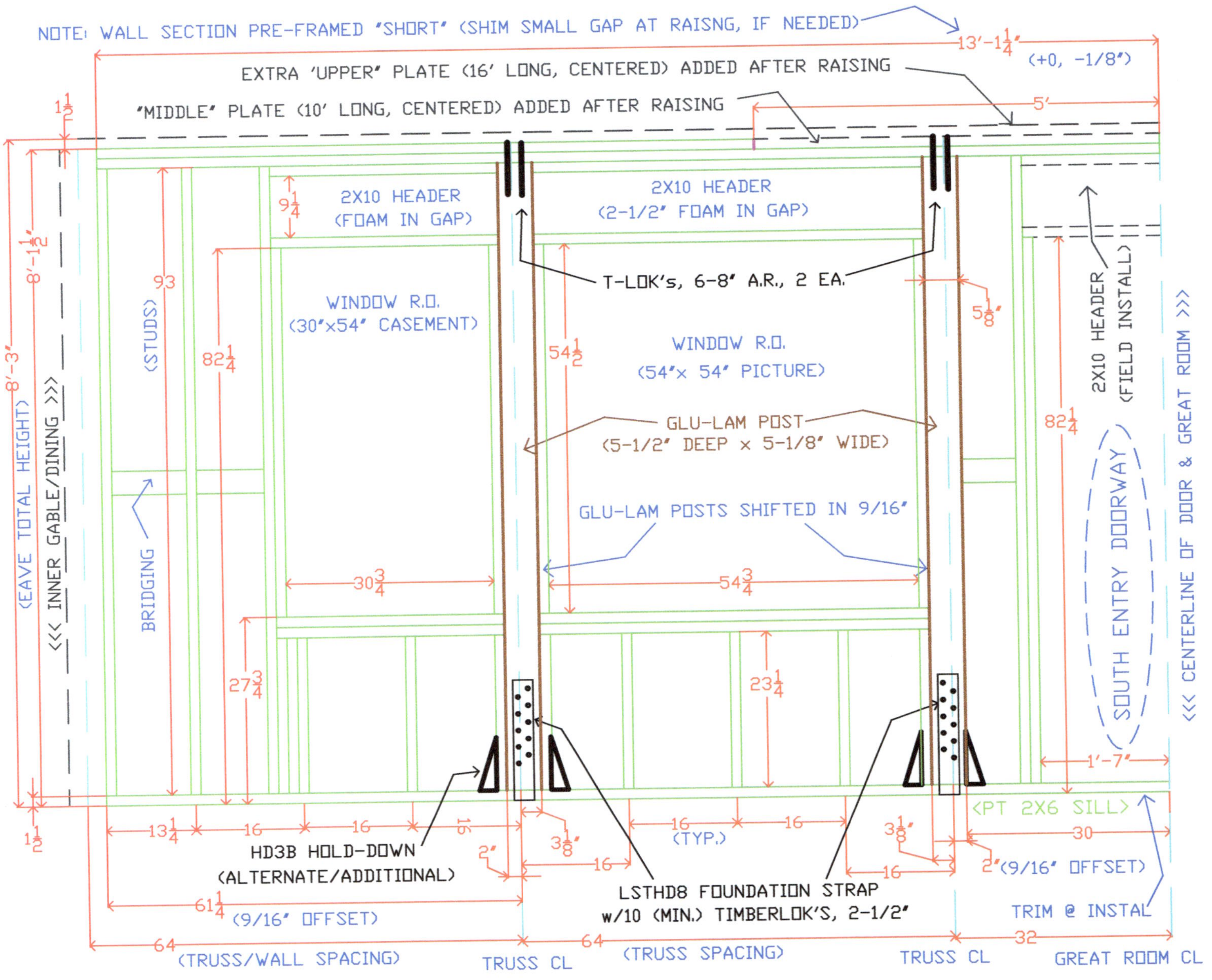

FIGURE 4.5 - SOUTH DINING FRAMED WALL

NOTE: The "Living" Zone wall is identical, symmetrical, and thus not shown

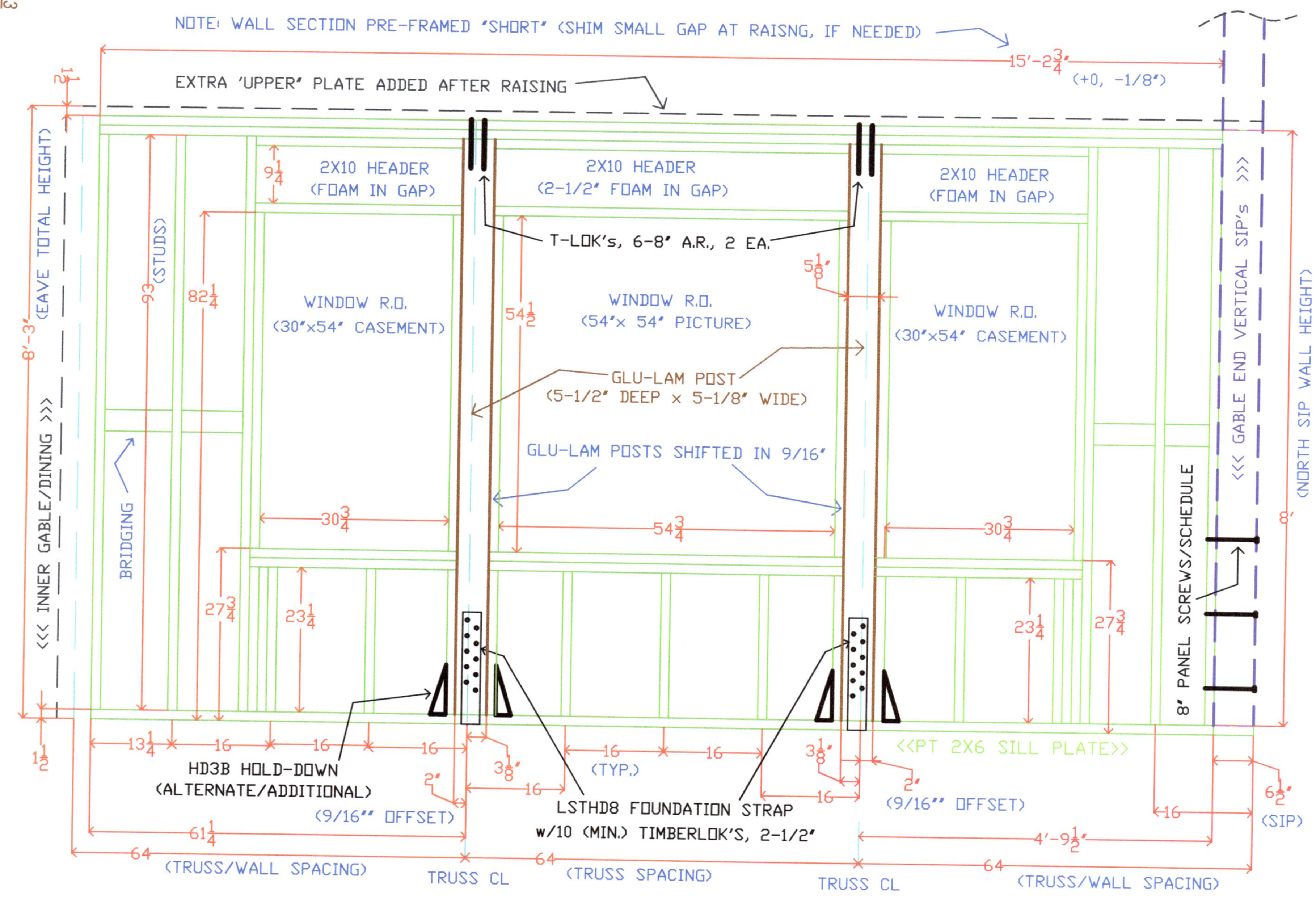

FIGURE 4.6 - SOUTH MASTER BEDROOM FRAMED WALL

(NORTH SIP WALL HEIGHT)

8'

(SIP) 6½"

<<< GABLE END VERTICAL SIP's >>>

8' PANEL SCREWS/SCHEDULE

2X10 HEADER (FOAM IN GAP)

WINDOW R.O. (30"x54" CASEMENT)

27¾

23¼

30¾

<<PT 2X6 SILL PLATE>>

2'

(9/16" OFFSET)

16

(TRUSS/WALL SPACING)

4'-9½'

64

(TRUSS/WALL SPACING)

TRUSS CL

15'-2¾' (+0, -1/8")

2X10 HEADER (2-1/2" FOAM IN GAP)

T-LOK's, 6-8" A.R., 2 EA.

5⅝"

WINDOW R.O. (54"x 54" PICTURE)

GLU-LAM POST (5-1/2" DEEP x 5-1/8" WIDE)

GLU-LAM POSTS SHIFTED IN 9/16"

54¾

54½

LSTHD8 FOUNDATION STRAP w/10 (MIN.) TIMBERLOK's, 2-1/2"

3⅛"

16

16

16

(TYP.)

16

64

(TRUSS SPACING)

TRUSS CL

NOTE: WALL SECTION PRE-FRAMED 'SHORT' (SHIM SMALL GAP AT RAISING, IF NEEDED)

EXTRA 'UPPER' PLATE ADDED AFTER RAISING

2X10 HEADER (FOAM IN GAP)

WINDOW R.O. (30"x54" CASEMENT)

9¼

30¾

23¼

27¾

82¼

93 (STUDS)

BRIDGING

61¼

13¼

16

16

16

3⅛"

2'

(9/16" OFFSET)

64

(TRUSS/WALL SPACING)

HD3B HOLD-DOWN (ALTERNATE/ADDITIONAL)

1½

(EAVE TOTAL HEIGHT)

<<< INNER GABLE/DINING >>>

8'-3'

1½

23

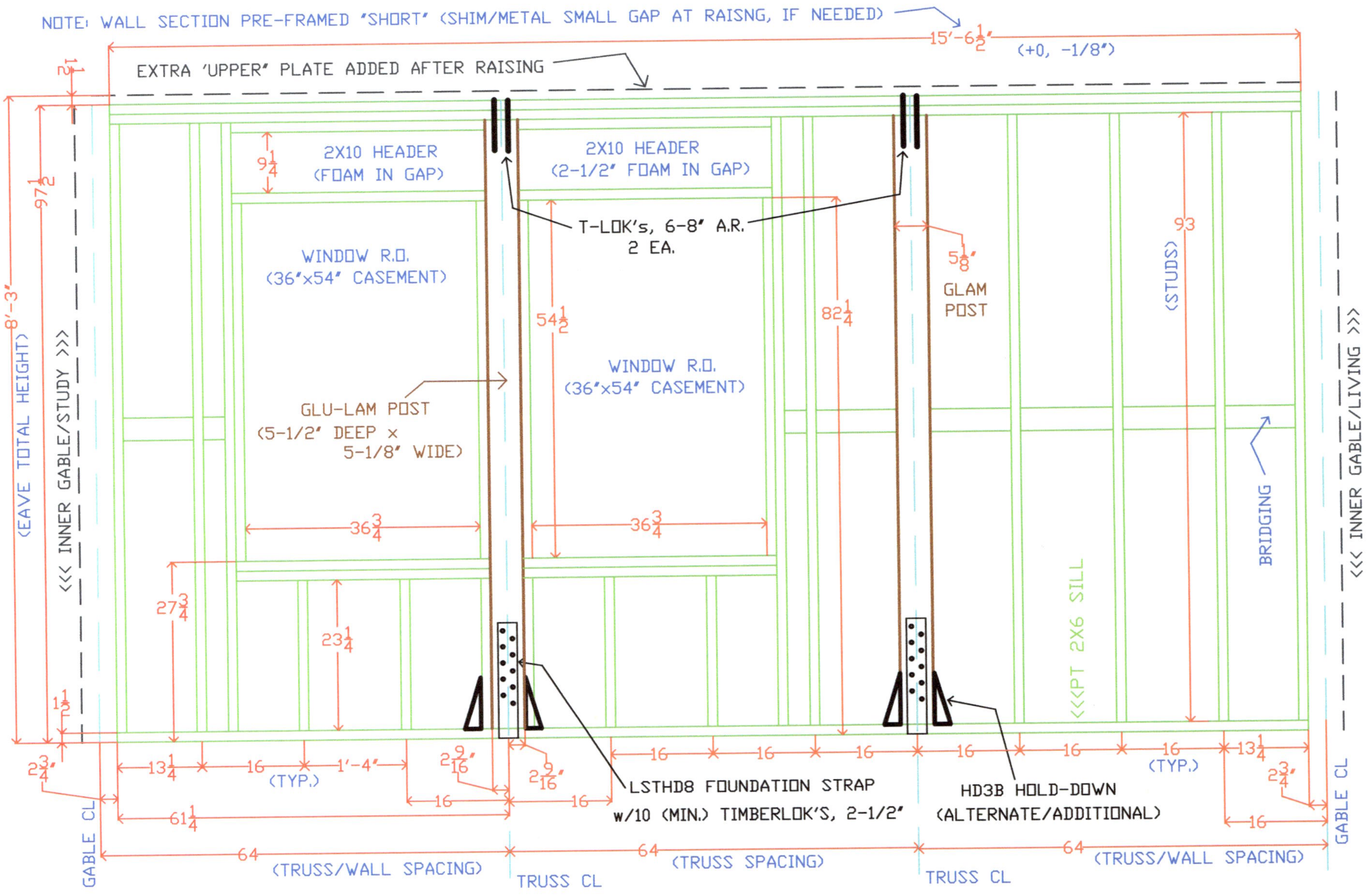

FIGURE 4.7 - SOUTH GUEST BEDROOM FRAMED WALL

<<< INNER GABLE/LIVING >>>

GABLE CL

BRIDGING

93 (STUDS)

<<< PT 2X6 SILL

(+0, −1/8")

15'-6½"

GLAM POST

5⅝

2X10 HEADER
(2-1/2" FOAM IN GAP)

T-LOK's, 6-8" A.R.
2 EA.

82¼

HD3B HOLD-DOWN
(ALTERNATE/ADDITIONAL)

TRUSS CL

(TRUSS/WALL SPACING)

64

16

16 (TYP.)

13¼

2¾

16

16

16

16

16

16

16

16

WINDOW R.O.
(36"x54" CASEMENT)

36¾

54½

LSTHD8 FOUNDATION STRAP
w/10 (MIN.) TIMBERLOK'S, 2-1/2"

TRUSS CL

(TRUSS SPACING)

64

NOTE: WALL SECTION PRE-FRAMED 'SHORT' (SHIM/METAL SMALL GAP AT RAISING, IF NEEDED)

EXTRA 'UPPER' PLATE ADDED AFTER RAISING

2X10 HEADER
(FOAM IN GAP)

9¼

WINDOW R.O.
(36"x54" CASEMENT)

GLU-LAM POST
(5-1/2" DEEP x
5-1/8" WIDE)

36¾

23¼

27¾

13¼

61¼

TRUSS CL

(TRUSS/WALL SPACING)

64

(TYP.) 1'-4"

2 9/16"

2 9/16"

16

16

16

GABLE CL

<<< INNER GABLE/STUDY >>>

1½

1½

97½

2¾

(EAVE TOTAL HEIGHT)

8'-3"

24

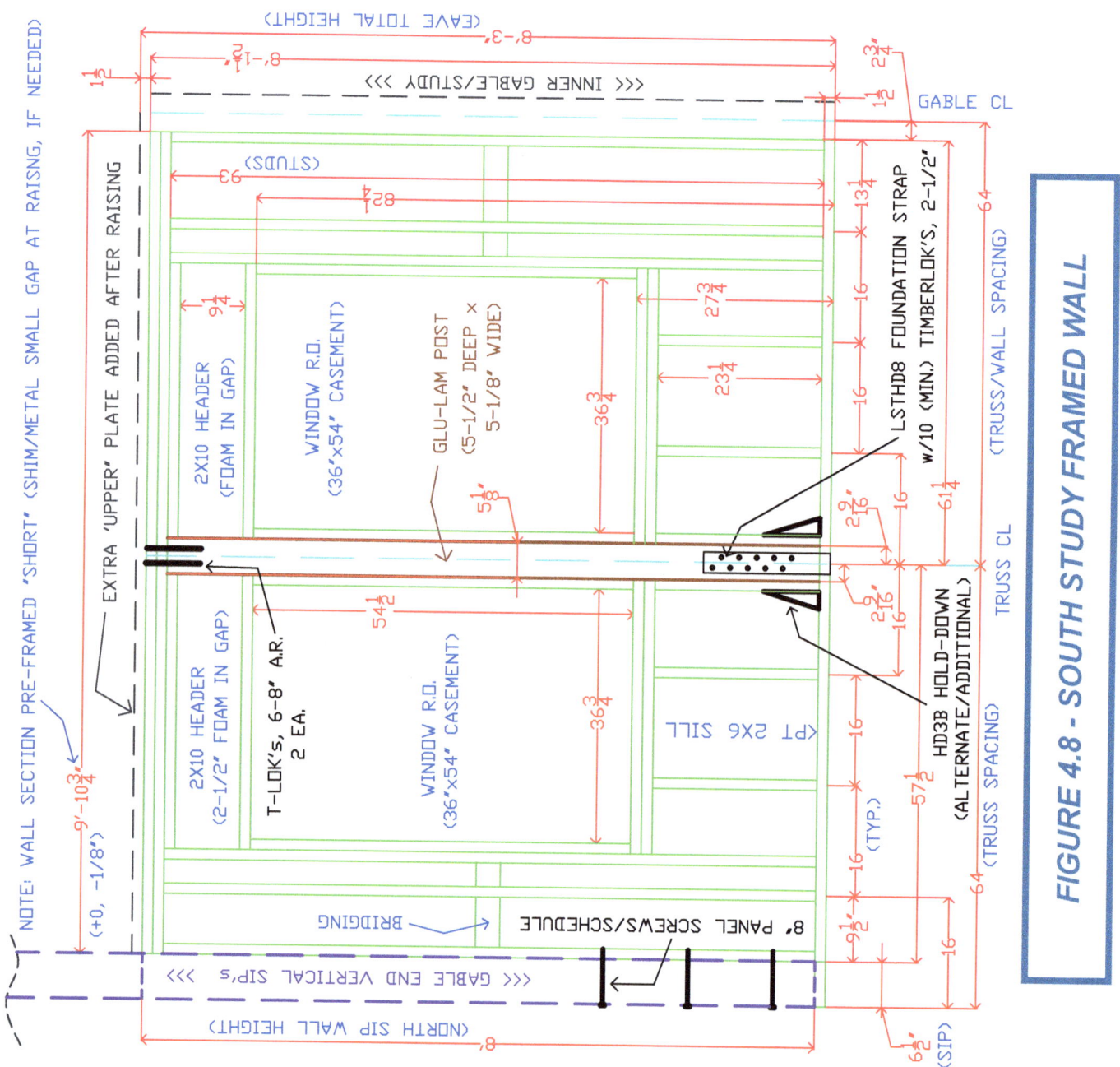

FIGURE 4.8 - SOUTH STUDY FRAMED WALL

FRAMED "INNER GABLE" WALL SECTIONS See Figure 4.9 next on page 27 >>>

The three inner-gable walls dividing the house up into the five major zones are framed, and since they are load-bearing on the same 64" pattern as the roof timber trusses, they are 2x6 based.

5 MAJOR SUB-COMPONENTS OF THE INNER GABLE WALLS:

1. NORTH HALF OF LOWER WALL
2. SOUTH HALF OF LOWER WALL (not identical to north)
3. SOUTH UPPER "QUADRANT"
4. NORTH UPPER "QUADRANT" (identical to south quadrant)
5. RIDGE POST (Glulam as in ridge beam & wall posts at south windows)

All four of these framed modules would be best built in advance in a shop. A good business investment, if volumes warranted, is fabricating steel table-height "tooling jigs" for rapid and consistent assembly for the three types of sections (North Lower & South Lower, even though not identical could utilize one jig.). Note the two *"quadrant"* halves (upper trapezoid wall sections that <u>must match the Timber truss profile</u>) are similar to those used in the prior *SIMPLE SIP* book which describes a tooling jig example for that version truss.

(See >SSIP, C3, P50, FIG3.7 & 3.8<)

Note that we also show this trusses' matching QUADRANT on the rear cover.

All four framed sections should be braced (temporary 2x4 diagonal) in the shop for structural integrity while moving. (All these gable related portions could transport on a medium load size 16 ft., <u>deck-over</u> trailer or a partial load on a longer 20-24 ft. version.)

After raising the two lower gable sections at the building site, adding a longer mid-spanning 2x6 "middle" top 12ft plate, plus the third top layer stiffens this, now long, inner gable wall .

The glulam ridge post provides a solid support for the glulam horizontal ridge beam (with 4/12 roof pitch shaped on top corners) that ties in the Timber Trusses to the inner (framed) & outer gable (SIP) walls. Two 8" TimberLOK's screws (minimum) through the ridge beams down into the post tops make a secure tie-in. The end vertical plate of the wedge shaped "Quadrants" nail also to the 6x6 sides after lifting on the wall. The second top plate for the quadrants can be added even before lifting in place. (only one plate in jig)

MISC. FRAMED 2x4 SECTIONS:

The several short in-fill 2x4 walls in the bedroom and study wings of the house that complete the bathrooms, closets, etc. are pretty standard framing and will not be covered here. The four short walls forming the kitchen pantry and coat closet are tied into fitting between the twin collar beams of the Timber Trusses. So, filling in these, and with some potential to customize the final sizes there, are best built at site. However, some of these walls could also benefit a jig-table scheme if production volumes warrant the shift to pre-fab work versus on-site-framing.

With the south pre-framed wall sections and the earlier SIP walls covered,

we can shift to discussing the next major structural sub-system:

The ROOF !

Now we will reveal in the next chapter why this Timber-Truss roof structure is so key . . .

(Maybe it might even protect your head one day?)

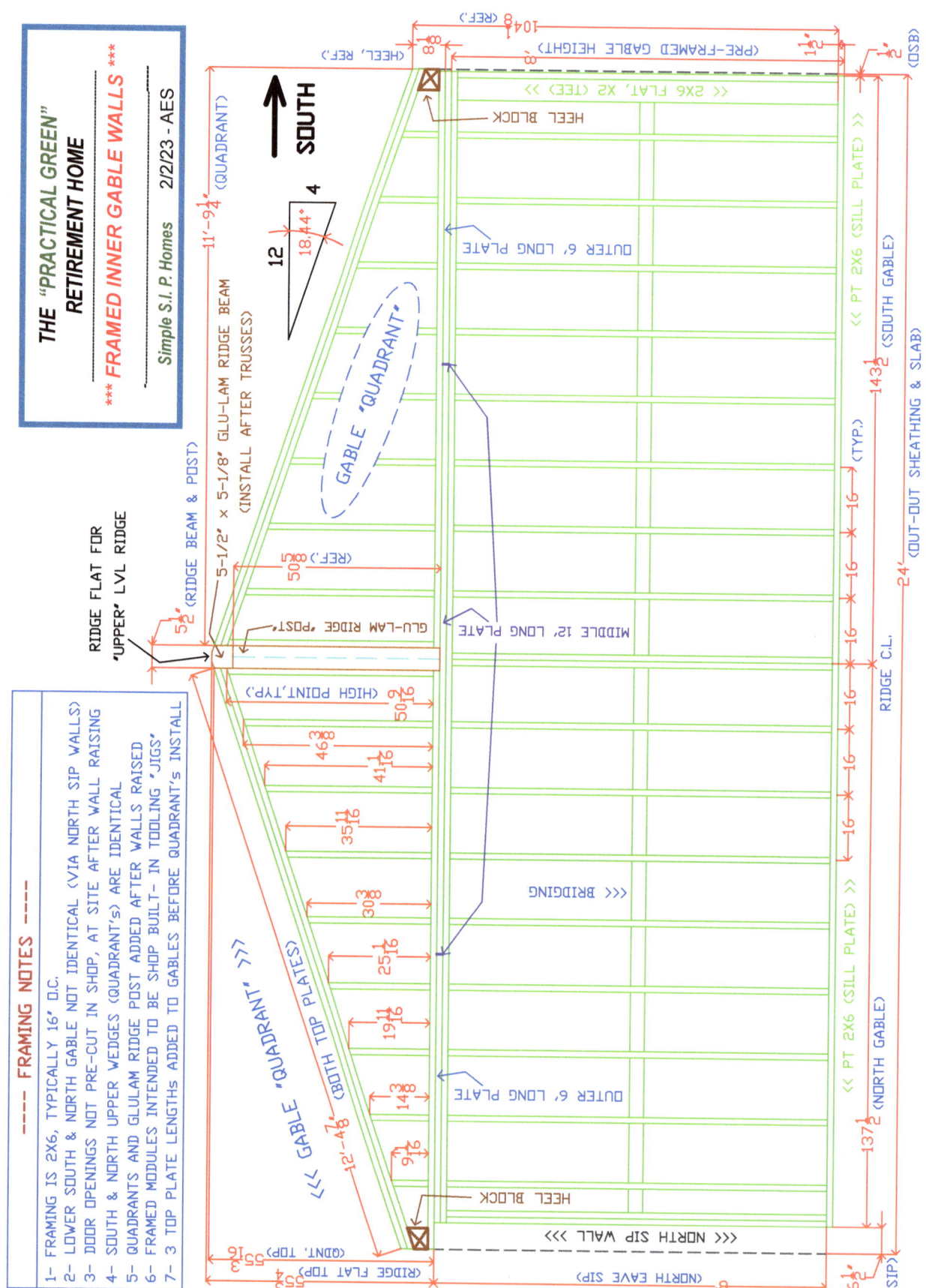

FIGURE 4.9 - FRAMED INNER GABLE WALLS

CHAPTER 5 – ROOF SYSTEM

American homeowners should realize that the typical 2x framed or even "PRE-FAB" trusses (usually with 2x4's) roof systems are really not adequate in higher-wind regions. Typically, they are only a 20# per s.f. loading, with some more for northern snow load regions. A key weakness is that the typical top sheathing is only 7/6" thick "OSB", nailed with about #10-12 size nails. (normal full "framing" nails are the larger #16) In high winds situations, these roofs typically "peel off" in small sections rather than remain intact as one large zone as we will now describe. Even the small, thin "hurricane" straps now in some higher wind zones, to hold the rafters down to the eave top plates, seem flimsey when you see our design element details.

Note again in the roof construction sequence photo, just after Figure 2.4, page 12, that our ridge system is a <u>dual-stacked-pair</u>. The Glulam beam seen inside the home at the top of the Timber Trusses (page 9 picture) and the "upper ridge" LVL engineered beam is above as exposed in the roof sequence picture. (is EPS gap) Our dual ridges spread the roof load, and if any impacts, spread across multiple trusses.

But: The 2x4 based, pre-made trusses, usually do <u>not have a center peak "Ridge beam"</u>. Likely only a row or two of horizontal 2x4 "bridging studs", <u>below the ridge</u>, that essentially just firm the truss spacing. Oh . . . those trusses are at a wider 24" centers, vs hand-framed 2x8, etc rafter roofs which are on 16" centers!

<u>Think about even a medium size tree hitting this OSB ridge top between the 2 ft truss gap!</u>

"QUEEN" 4/12-24ft TRUSS OVERVIEW   See Figure 5.1 next page >>>

- The Timber-Truss design uses a modern "engineered wood" material: Glue-laminated beams (or "Glu-Lams", Glulam, etc):
- Glulams typically use very strong **Southern Yellow Pine**, dried at the plant to low moisture
- Much stronger than the **Eastern White Pine**, locally available, wood used in the **Simple SIP House** book floor plans (glulam FB "bending" force rating of 2400# while EWP about 700 # ?)
- Standard size 2x4's (3-1/2" x 1-1/2") are planned to finish size of 3-1/8" wide & 1-3/8" thick per layer
- Layers are high-strength-glued under pressure to create different beam sizes
- Beam sizes are multiple 1-3/8" layers, thus our chosen sizes, & smaller than EWP 4x wood are: **Rafter & Kingpost** = 8-1/4" high (6 layers), **Collar** beams and angle **Webs** = 5-1/2" high (4 layers)

<u>The truss plates are ¼" thick plate steel</u>, likely laser cut, and typically flat black <u>powder-coated</u> finish. Regional area steel fabrication shops usually have either this preferred laser cutting, or water-jet, etc. technologies. With the complete mechanical drawings on each part, fabrication time and costs are typically reasonable. This only four different part types (**Top** plate, **Mid-collar** plate, angle **Web** plate, and the only bent part: **Base** bracket) totals to only 12 parts per truss. (should cost in the $200-$300 range per truss)

The miscellaneous hardware consists of only five types of parts (roughly $100 cost per truss):

1. 5/8"-11 bolts - 5" long, Grade #2, 12 each
2. 5/8"-11 bolts - 11" long, Grade #2 & #5, 5 each (but 2 truss end bolts should be Grade #5)
3. 5/8"-11 hex nuts, Grade #2, 17 each (2 are Grade 5)
4. 5/8" flat washers, 34 each (painted flat black to match truss plates)
5. 5/8" black plastic bolt/nut cover caps , 30 each (available online via Essentra Components)

This size Timber Truss is <u>reasonably easy to fabricate in a medium size shop</u> with just one 12" sliding compound saw, one deep-travel drill press (3-1/2" minimum) and tables to support the beam handling. My prior business, before retiring, **Rocky Ridge Designs**', truss shop was set up for efficient production with twin saws about 12 feet apart and two drill presses just outboard of the saws and with table rollers. Two workers typically could fabricate each of the rafter and collar beams in the 10-12 minute time frame (about 3-4 cuts, 3-5 holes, ¾" dia., drilled). The slightly more complex center King Post with the two bandsaw notches for the rafter top seats added some fabrication time. Even with an extra edge router finish (about 1/4" to 3/8" radius, per preferred "look") and sanding, the entire labor per truss was in the 2-3 hour range.

We designed (CAD) "tool plates" from thin 1/16" steel with the beam outline and hole center locations for quick & accurate beam layout. Again, more modern "production techniques" not usual in hand-framed, built-at-site, homes were utilized in our operation. (I co-oped at aircraft plant in engineering school !)

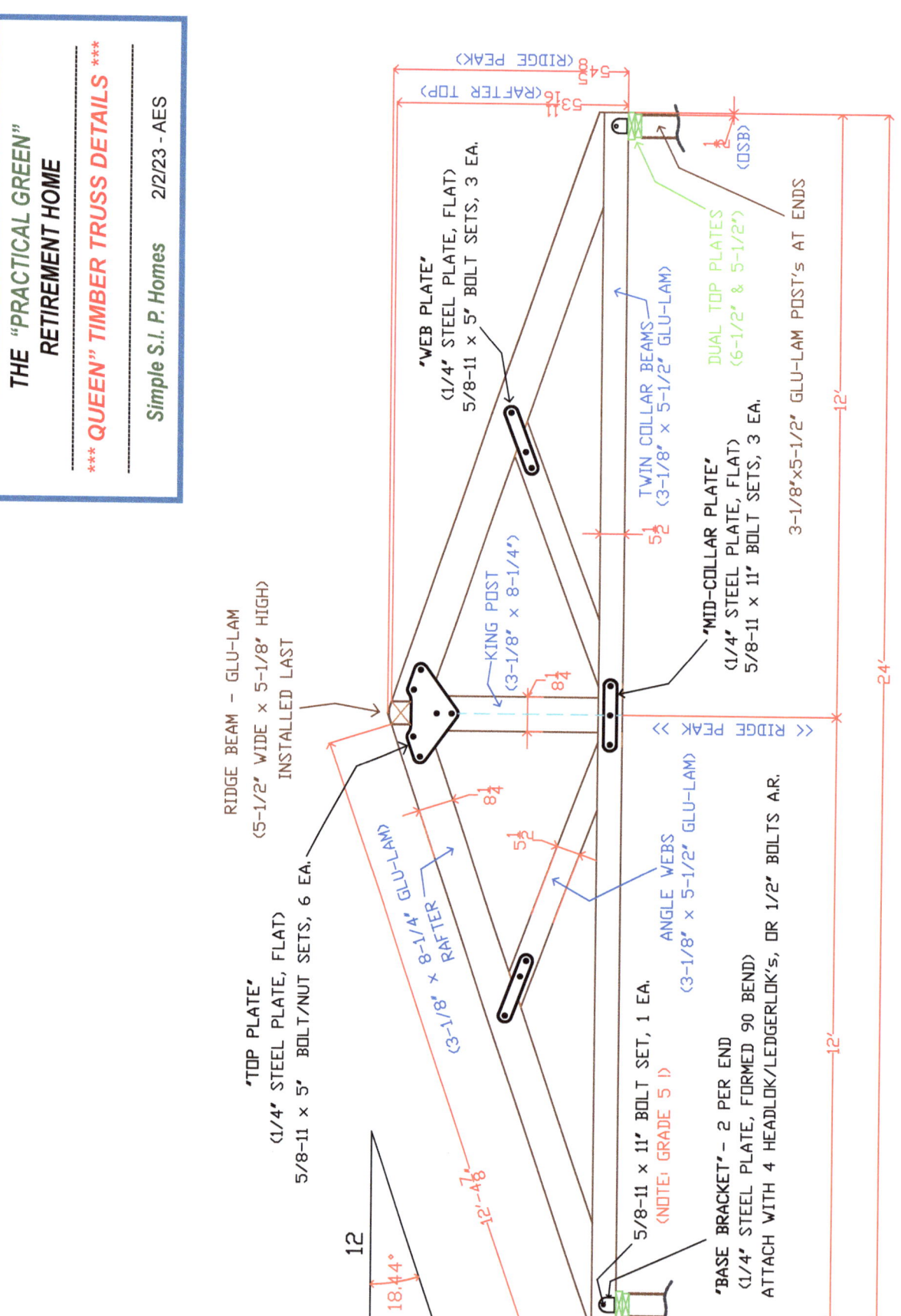

FIGURE 5.1 - "QUEEN" TIMBER TRUSS DETAILS

'TOP PLATE'
(1/4" STEEL PLATE, FLAT)
5/8-11 × 5" BOLT/NUT SETS, 6 EA.

RIDGE BEAM – GLU-LAM
(5-1/2" WIDE × 5-1/8" HIGH)
INSTALLED LAST

'WEB PLATE'
(1/4" STEEL PLATE, FLAT)
5/8-11 × 5" BOLT SETS, 3 EA.

KING POST
(3-1/8" × 8-1/4")

TWIN COLLAR BEAMS
(3-1/8" × 5-1/2" GLU-LAM)

DUAL TOP PLATES
(6-1/2" & 5-1/2")

(OSB)

3-1/8"×5-1/2" GLU-LAM POST's AT ENDS

'MID-COLLAR PLATE'
(1/4" STEEL PLATE, FLAT)
5/8-11 × 11" BOLT SETS, 3 EA.

(3-1/8" × 8-1/4" GLU-LAM)
RAFTER

ANGLE WEBS
(3-1/8" × 5-1/2" GLU-LAM)

5/8-11 × 11" BOLT SET, 1 EA.
(NOTE: GRADE 5 !)

'BASE BRACKET' – 2 PER END
(1/4" STEEL PLATE, FORMED 90 BEND)
ATTACH WITH 4 HEADLOK/LEDGERLOK's, OR 1/2" BOLTS A.R.

<< RIDGE PEAK >>

(RAFTER TOP)

(RIDGE PEAK)

12

4

18.44°

12'-7 4/8"

6 5/8"
(HEEL)

53 11/16
54 8

8 1/4

8 1/4

5 1/2

5 1/2

12'

12'

24'

ROOF DETAILS IN "SECTION VIEW"

See Figure 4.2 next page >>>

With strong Timber Trusses (likely much above 30 lb/sf rating, local P.E.should check) the key component in our roof system, the other elements are detailed in the following "Section View" of this home. (A section view is a "slice-thru cut" of a building revealing internal details)

CEILING DECKING (visible inside ceiling, is the final finish material, already) :

* Typically **Eastern White Pine** 2x6 (or 8) **T&G** (**T**onque & **G**roove) wood decking at 16 ft. long
* Enables alternating per row, "interlacing", with 64", 128", & 196" pattern
* Nail (#16's, 2-3 ea.) T&G right on timber truss "rafters" & gable walls (care for exposed nails)
* Cover finished T&G top with good underlayment ("Titanium")
* Typical suppliers indicate roof ratings in the 45-55 # per square ft. range (check local P.E.)

FOAM PANELS:

* Roof insulation = EPS, two layers of 4-5/8" thick (R18.5 ea, total = R37), "Full" roof = R39
* Stagger horizontal and vertical joints (thus, some 2'x8' panels & normal 4'x8' size)
* Tightly fit panels, use foam industry type <u>hot-wire cutting</u> tool, **<u>not framing saws</u> !!**
* 4'x8' table, with 90 degree & 4/12 roof pitch steel angle guides expedite cutting

TOP SHEATHING:

* Prefer ½" CDX plywood vs 7/16" OSB (could be thicker depending on SIP screw used)
* Use 11" SIP panel screws, 3x3 pattern (per 4x8) with torque limited, hand power drills (test to establish torque setting to not over-pull the CDX plywood down too much)
* Care to not hit T&G bottom V-groove and not punch through the T&G interior surface (only ¼" spare for 11" panel screw, thus screw 1-1/4" into 1-1/2" T&G wood depth)
* Effectively, the <u>9 SIP screws per sheet</u> form a strong "sandwich" very much like SIP panels, but the strong screws (about a ton per sheet hold-down) is like the glue in the SIP factory The #16 nails for the 2x T&G to the Glulam beams (36 min. per sheet) are about 100 # each = almost 2 tons per sheet plywood sheet area (x 60 sheets !), mates with the CDX hold

TOP SURFACE MEMBRANE COVER:

* Strongly recommend W.R. Grace "**Ice & Watershield**" ® covering the entire top sheathing
* Or: good "equivalent" membrane product (But, much better than typical cheap black felt !)
* Likely installed cost is the $1.70 - $2.00 per sq. ft. range

PREFERRED "SANDWICH BUILD-UP" vs LARGE ROOF SIP's APPROACH:

* This "Build-Up" layer system with 1-1/2" thick T&G ceiling likely stronger than roof SIP's
* Roof SIP's typically in the $10-$13 per sf range
* This sandwich approach costs in similar, if not less, price range (factor in the inside finish)
* When T&G wood decking installed, a large <u>interior finish</u> (ceiling) step is <u>already done</u> !
* SIP roofs using sheetrock under may even be costlier (labor for cut/fit/trim-out, etc.)
* And, using thinner 1-by's T&G <u>nailed under</u> is even higher labor costs (& not "structural")
* Fitting & handling (more boom truck time) for the longer 24 ft. SIP <u>roof</u> panels has been more time consuming than first assumed <u>in actual practice</u>
* However, a smaller, budget-conscious "starter" home, a SIP ceiling with a lower cost ceiling covering (maybe thin T-111 textured plywood?) would then better fit that situation

After studying the Section View roof structure details . . .

Then, after, we divide up the house into five zones and detail significant points next :

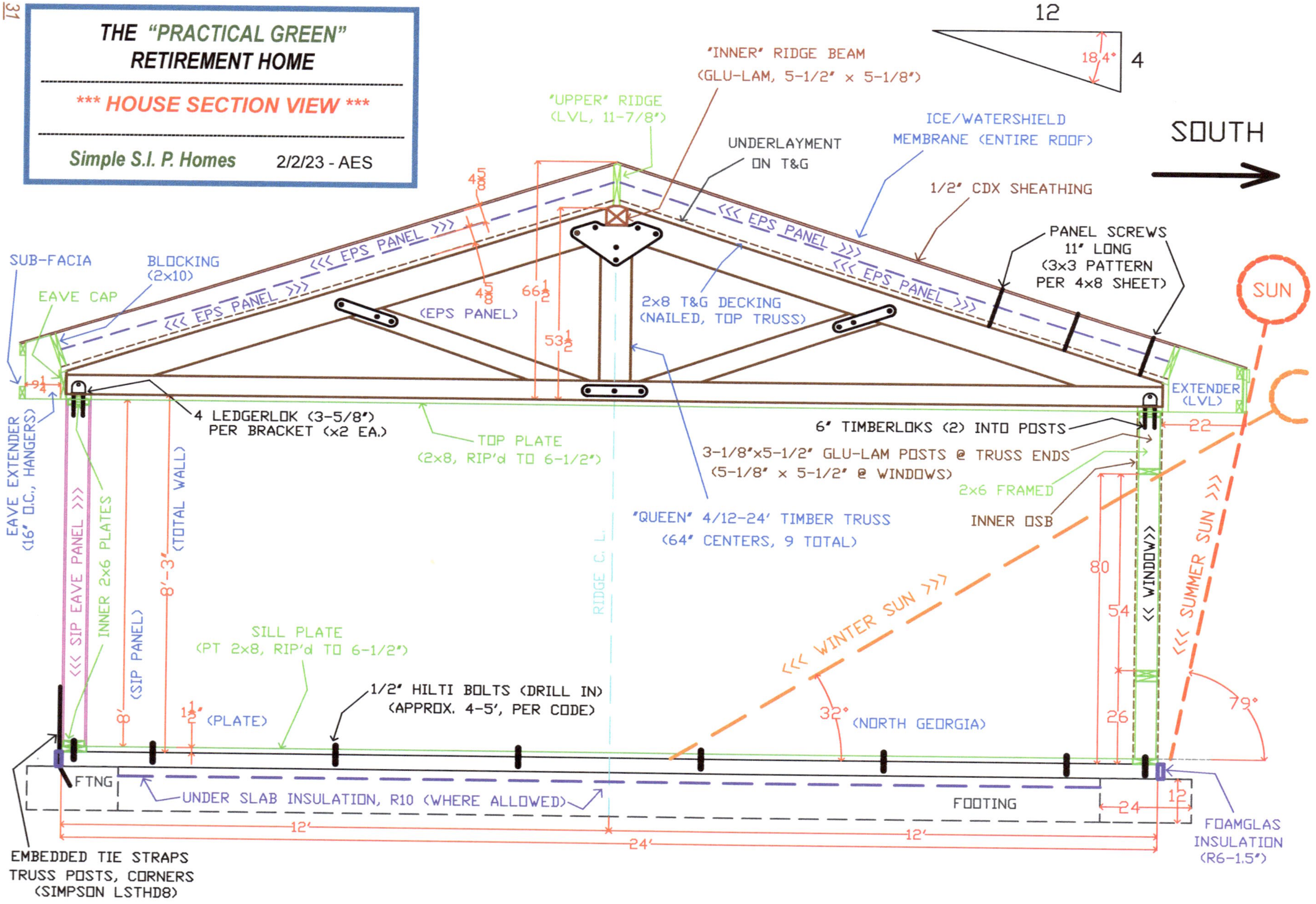

SOUTH

SUN

SUMMER SUN >>>

<<< WINTER SUN >>>

12
4
18.4°

'INNER' RIDGE BEAM
(GLU-LAM, 5-1/2" × 5-1/8")

ICE/WATERSHIELD MEMBRANE (ENTIRE ROOF)

1/2" CDX SHEATHING

PANEL SCREWS 11" LONG (3×3 PATTERN PER 4×8 SHEET)

UNDERLAYMENT ON T&G

<<< EPS PANEL >>>

EXTENDER (LVL)

<<WINDOW>>

FOAMGLAS INSULATION (R6-1.5")

79°

12

54
80
26
24

6" TIMBERLOKS (2) INTO POSTS

2×6 FRAMED

INNER OSB

32° (NORTH GEORGIA)

3-1/8"×5-1/2" GLU-LAM POSTS @ TRUSS ENDS
(5-1/8" × 5-1/2" @ WINDOWS)

'QUEEN" 4/12-24' TIMBER TRUSS
(64" CENTERS, 9 TOTAL)

12'

2×8 T&G DECKING (NAILED, TOP TRUSS)

'UPPER' RIDGE (LVL, 11-7/8")

53½
66½

RIDGE C.L.

(EPS PANEL)

TOP PLATE (2×8, RIP'd TO 6-1/2")

45 7/8
45 7/8

24'

4 5/8

12'

1/2" HILTI BOLTS (DRILL IN)
(APPROX. 4-5', PER CODE)

<<< EPS PANEL >>>

THE "PRACTICAL GREEN"
RETIREMENT HOME
*** HOUSE SECTION VIEW ***
Simple S.I.P. Homes   2/2/23 - AES

SILL PLATE
(PT 2×8, RIP'd TO 6-1/2")

UNDER SLAB INSULATION, R10 (WHERE ALLOWED)

SUB-FACIA

EAVE CAP

BLOCKING (2×10)

4 LEDGERLOK (3-5/8")
PER BRACKET (×2 EA.)

EAVE EXTENDER (16" O.C., HANGERS)

4 5/8

<<< SIP EAVE PANEL >>>

INNER 2×6 PLATES

1½ (PLATE)

1½"

8'-3' (TOTAL WALL)

8' (SIP PANEL)

FTNG

FOOTING

EMBEDDED TIE STRAPS
TRUSS POSTS, CORNERS
(SIMPSON LSTHD8)

31

FIGURE 5.2 - SECTION VIEW OF HOUSE

CHAPTER 6 - FLOOR PLAN "ZONE" DETAILS

USING THE "ZOOMED-in-by- ZONE" CONCEPT FOR MORE DETAILS IN THE FLOOR PLAN:

First, we'll split the house into five zones with a fairly detailed drawing for each section on the right side of the book and the matching text " COMMENTS" on the left page when "spread" to both pages. Note these upcoming drawings show the interaction of typical furniture, doors, windows, critical spacings (rounded off to nearest inch) that can't be easily shown in busy typical "construction drawings".

(See Appendix 3 for potentially more technical construction information)

The importance here is that many homeowners buy homes and find out later that there are problems fitting their own or even typical furniture into the new home. This focusing concept aids in demonstrating the key trade-off points of construction realities coupled with typical furniture sizing, and then the resulting "spacings" or walk areas.

In general, the abbreviated text for comments page will be broken down into two subjects:

GENERAL COMMENTS:

1- Description of major appliances & typical sized furniture

2- Coding text on window type & size:

> C30-54 = Casement style, 30" wide, 54" tall
> A36-18 = Awning style, 36" wide, 18' high
> P54-54 = Picture (or "fixed, non-opening) 54" wide, 54" tall

PS: Do not recommend double-hung style and any decorative grilles (blocks view)

3- *Key or unusual feature notes point to detail (like "Magic" clothes hamper in Master Bath)*

4- *Generally, we are not focused here on a fully certified "Handicap" home, which likely requires a much larger footprint.*
(However, the Master Bedroom/Bath area is about the ballpark size of those needs.)

CONSTRUCTION NOTES:

1- *More construction details flagged in the Zone drawings*

2- *Specific pointers indicate more of the interactions of the three main building "modules"*

(SIP Panel walls, 2x6 framed walls, and Timber-Truss roof)

3- *Some details also note why certain devices located (like HVAC Mini-Split Indoor units)*

4- *Some construction "TIPs" indicate improving fabricating time efficiency, sequence, quality, etc.*

Now we can delve into the five house zones in even more detail:

GENERAL COMMENTS:

BEDROOM:

- WINDOWS: Triple-set, large center "Picture" (fixed), flanking casements (venting & egress)
- On south side for passive solar gain and medium height (54") for overhang shading
- Very reasonable spacings, easy movement flow around bed, bath, & closet doors
- Indoor mini-split HVAC at 45 angle utilizes nearby wall Kitchen "UTILITY CHASES"

BATHROOM:

- Large corner shower (only bath-<u>tub</u> in guest zone)
- Double sink vanity (60")
- Clothes hamper & linen integrated in tall cabinet (note "Magic" rear door in closet)

CLOSET:

- "**HIS**" & "**HER**" clothes hanging sides, shelves above (only 6-7' high), use vaulted space
- Washed/dryer stacked in rear middle (Hot water heater in blind corner)
- Rear door added to hamper for soiled laundry retrieval & clean linen access ("Magic Door")
- Modest custom corner counter-top (practical material, not granite, etc.), aids laundry tasks
- Shelf above counter and pull-out drawers below, enhance storage options

CONSTRUCTION NOTES:

1. East gable wall is 3 <u>vertical</u> SIP Panel <u>section</u> with Glulam posts (3-1/8" x 5-1/2") at joints
2. 3 Panel set laid out on Great Room slab floor & assembled before boom truck lift day
3. North SIP EAVE walls are 8ft. high by 64" wide, "<u>corner</u>" is 57-1/2", "<u>dual</u>" is 128" wide
4. 3-1/8" X 5-1/2" Glulam posts at Timber truss load point (64" centers) & joint points for SIP's
5. Thus, SIP foam reliefs at the smaller 3-1/8" wide posts = 1-9/16" (1/2 the post width)
6. At "large south window" 2x6 framed sections, posts are the larger 5-1/8" wide x 5-1/2" deep
7. "End Plates" = 2x6's foam reliefs in SIP ends are 1-1/2", normal sheathing nailing
8. Panel screws, per schedule rules, typically 8" long, at SIP corner junctions, etc.
9. Top & bottom 1-1/2" foam reliefs for inserted 2 x 6's to be flush with OSB 8ft ends
10. With PT 2x8 plate on slab, ripped to 6-1/2" plus extra ripped 2x8 top, <u>eave</u> wall height = 8'-3"
11. South wall is pre-framed 2x6 (in shop?) with outer OSB, but inner OSB layer is later, after spray foam insulation (recommend R22, low density/"open cell") & inspection after that
12. Windows = triple pane, prefer metal clad or fiberglass, LOW- E, but . . .
13. <u>Not have Solar-Gain prohibiting coating</u>, want Passive Solar gain in winter months (proper length roof overhang shades window in summer months) **> BTGH, C2, P99<**
14. Continuing 12x12 utility chase from kitchen thru bath to closet enables plumbing runs, wiring, mounting locations for bath exhaust vent & **ERV** (**E**nergy **R**ecovery **V**entilator)
15. The chase carrying most of the thru-house wiring runs also <u>minimizes</u> much of wiring in SIPs
16. Recommend Panasonic bath exhaust fan, model FV-0511VF1
17. Recommend Panasonic ERV is EnergyStar rated, model FV-06E1
18. Recommend "Marathon" ® lifetime water heater, by Rheem, is electric, <u>not gas!</u>

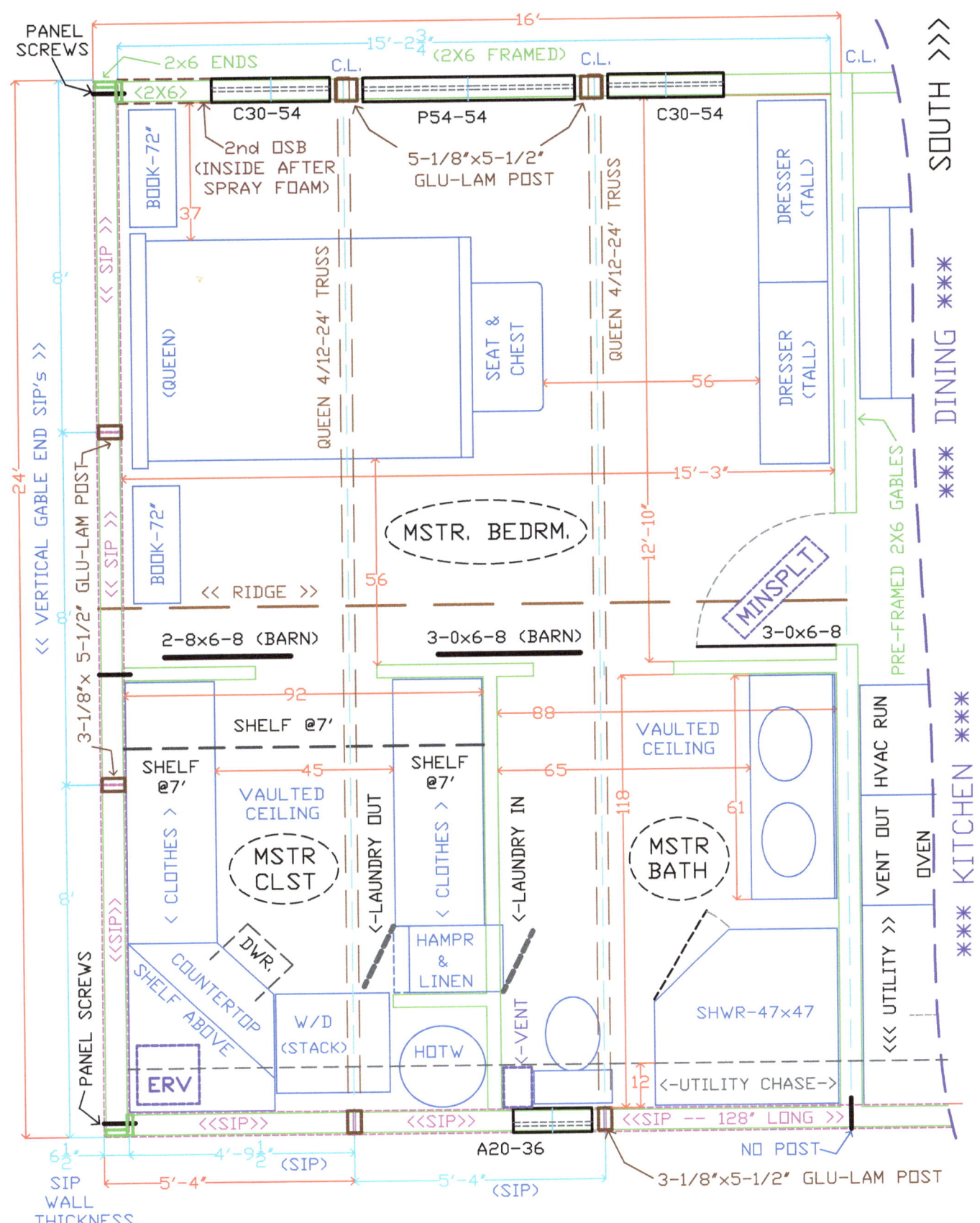

FIGURE 6.1 - "MASTER" BEDROOM ZONE DETAILS

KITCHEN - DINING ZONE

See Figure 6.2 opposite, page 36 >>>

GENERAL COMMENTS:

DINING:

- <u>WINDOWS:</u> large center "Picture" with flanking left/East casement (venting)
- Substantial east gable wall space for hutch & dish storage unit
- Even custom long 7ft. table, matched with "reasonable" bar counter depth = good seating
- Extra room on west enables Living room sofa shift to dining zone than indicated
- South (Deck) door is EnergyStar rated, clad steel, foam filled, with <u>only upper</u> half glass

KITCHEN:

- Awning style window over north wall sink
- Good sink is stainless steel "Farmers" 60/40 split with "custom" rear <u>drain panel below</u> counter surface (avoid the typical $200 plus "cutout fee" and thin/fragile back zone in counters)
- Rear stainless steel custom plate enables better sponge/soap storage & drainage (under top) (S.S. = 36"x8", two 90 bends, 2" up back , 1-1/2" down front, 4-1/2" flat & plumb hole)
- Pull-out trash tray in base near dead corner (leave dead corner for utility access??)
- 22 c.f. refrigerator shown near pantry, if want larger 25-26cf, reduce base 18" cabinet
- Pull out drawers in bases flanking oven most useful:
  - ➢ Left = two pot/pan drawers, 14" each high, or 12" & 16" ?
  - ➢ Right = 3 drawers, like 5", 10", & 13" high (forks, etc.)
- Exhaust vent is EnergyStar rated, low profile, not "fancy" shape that loses upper cabinet space

CONSTRUCTION NOTES:

1. East gable wall is framed 2x6 (best pre-framed in shop) in halves, erected at site w/Quadrants
2. North SIP walls are 8ft. high by 64" wide, and dual 128" wide panel sections
3. 3-1/8" X 5-1/2" GLULAM posts at Timber truss load point (64" centers) & joint points for SIP's
4. Thus, SIP foam reliefs at the smaller 3-1/8" wide posts = 1-9/16" (1/2 the post width)
5. At wide south window 2x6 framed sections, posts are the larger 5-1/8" wide x 5-1/2" deep
6. Panel screws used per schedule rules, typically 8" long, at SIP corner junctions, etc.
7. Top & bottom reliefs are for 2x6 "inserted" to be flush with OSB 8ft. heights
8. With PT 2x8 plate on slab, ripped to 6-1/2" plus extra ripped 2x8 top= wall height 8'-3"
9. South wall is pre-framed 2x6 (in shop prior?) with outer OSB, but inner OSB layer is installed later, after spray foam insulation (recommend R22, low density/"open cell") & then inspection
10. Windows = triple pane, prefer metal clad or fiberglass, LOW- E, but not have the Solar-Gain prohibiting for Passive Solar gain in winter (roof overhang shades in summer months)
11. Continuing 12x12 utility chase from kitchen thru bath to closet enables long wiring runs, HVAC plumbing runs, and locations for bath exhaust vent & **ERV** (**E**nergy **R**ecover **V**entilator)
12. The 7 ft bottom of the Utility chase also mates well with the typical kitchen cabinet top height (Best not to have taller 8 ft. cabinets with elderly occupants - safer level to reach!)
13. Recommend brands like Panasonic for exhaust vents - EnergyStar rated

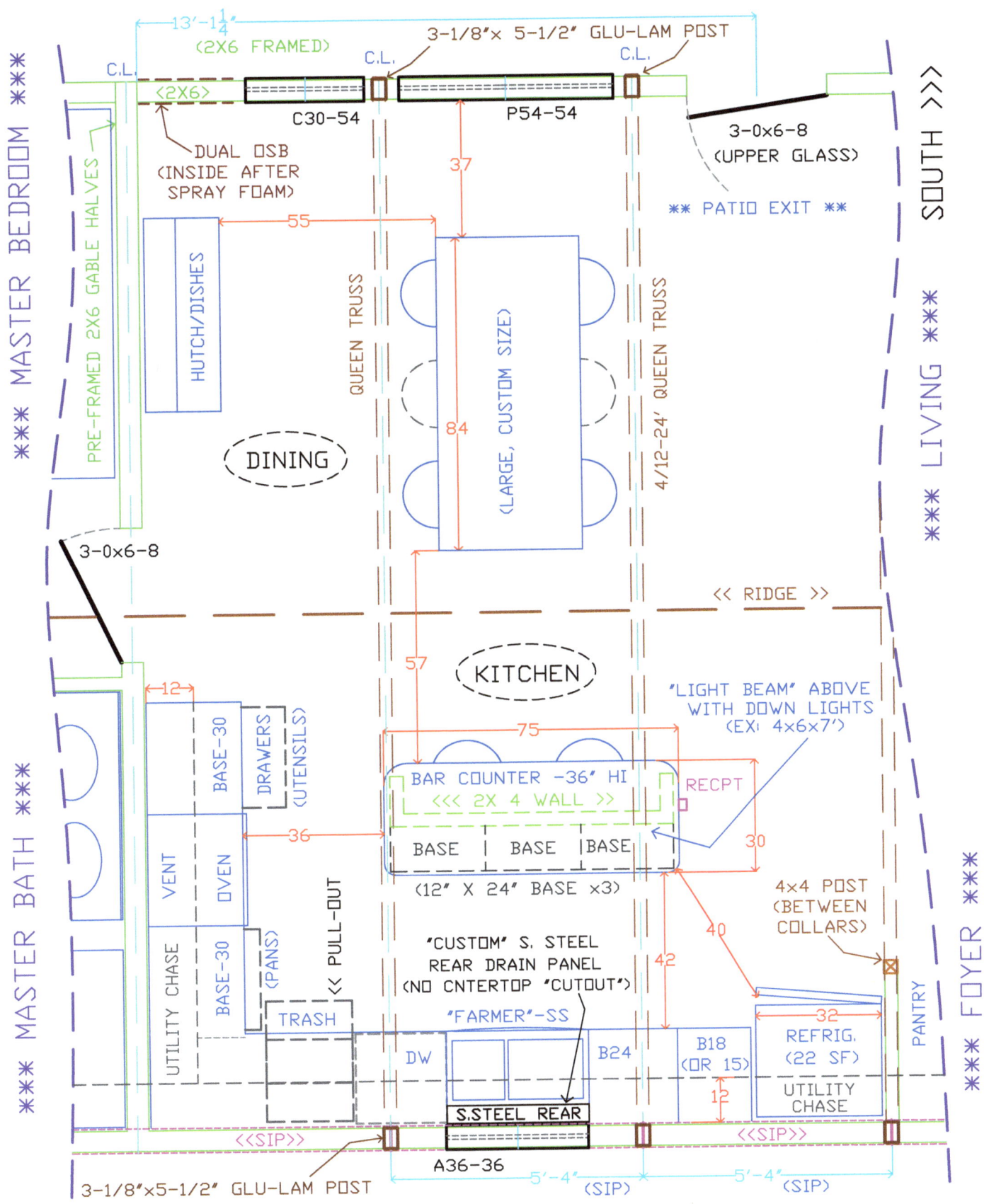

FIGURE 6.2 - KITCHEN/DINING ZONE DETAILS

LIVING ZONE

See Figure 6.3 opposite, page 38 >>>

GENERAL COMMENTS:

LIVING:

- <u>WINDOWS:</u> large center "Picture" with flanking right/West casement (venting)
- Substantial west gable wall length for wood stove, book case, & TV mounting
- Two chair (@ 45 degrees) flanking center sofa optimal for TV view & wood stove
- "Modest size" recliners could also fit in chair locations with some spacing impact
- Sofa/Chair location actually can shift more to dining table (EAST) than shown here
- Space from chair to coats/pantry may enable more room for guest/Foyer entry
- TV low bookcase could increase to 16" deep for better TV location & more storage
- <u>Wood stove:</u>
    >Small efficient, <u>sealed glass door</u> version, with <u>outside</u> combustion air intake
    > Recommend Englander NV17L ($1000 ?), also for emergency cooking

WOOD STOVE & BRICK SURROUND:

- Brick "surround" = thermal mass & safe buffer (curtains): 48" wide, 24" deep, about 53" high
- Can elevate about 12" with steel angle lintels (2"x3/16" x 36", 2 ea.)
- Fiber-cement 1x12 "board" as door over bottom zone (smaller firewood storage there also)
- Wood box, log sized, between surround and south wall hides 3" air intake pipe
- Air in pipe sits on PT sill in south wall, makes 90 bend under stove
- Wood box base = two lengths of 4x6 PT (5-1/2" high) to lift box bottom over pipe
- Tall, narrow,(18" x 4-5' ?) book case(s) flanking low bookcase (24-30" high, 5 ft long ?) , enables good TV viewing location (up to 60-65" diagonal screen?)

PANTRY & COAT CLOSET :

- Pantry corners are 4x4 pine posts (trim top to 3-1/8") & attach within truss collars
- Pantry can go 4-6" deeper if living room chair space still adequate ?
- Pantry shelves: <u>side</u> = 16" deep (& tall gap, for bulky), <u>rear</u> = 6" (cans & thin boxes, 1-2 deep)
- Pantry <u>non-shelf side</u> is good location for hang-up brooms, mops, utensils, etc.
- Ceiling T&G decking on truss collars enables "Utility chase function" to bath
- Coat's door is wide (36") bi-fold (good coat access, but minimal impact on foyer space)

FOYER :

- Avoid temptation to use <u>oversize</u> table at entry door corner (mail, keys, notes, etc)
- Best = 8"x24" wall-mounted shelves (2+?), 45 angle cut end (see magenta dashed line)
- Even more lower shelves could store pair-shoes-each?
- Wall covering/picture, etc can hide the electrical panel just above these shelves

CONSTRUCTION NOTES:

1. South Wall is pre-framed (shop?) 2x6 in exact half sections, header left free
2. After both halves in place, door header, jack studs & longer "upper" plate installed
3. Extra inner OSB layer installed after spray foam & relevant inspection
4. Gable wall section (West) pre-framed 2x6's, note North & South different lengths
5. North & south gables frame identical, with specific door openings cut in after install
6. "Quadrant" 4/12 slope tops & Glulam ridge posts installed on gable walls, before truss lift
7. North wall = 64" wide by 8' high SIP's with 3-1/8" glulam posts at truss ends/joints
8. Extra 2x8 top plate (rip'd to 6-1/2") on SIP's provides 3" thick truss base plate mounting surface

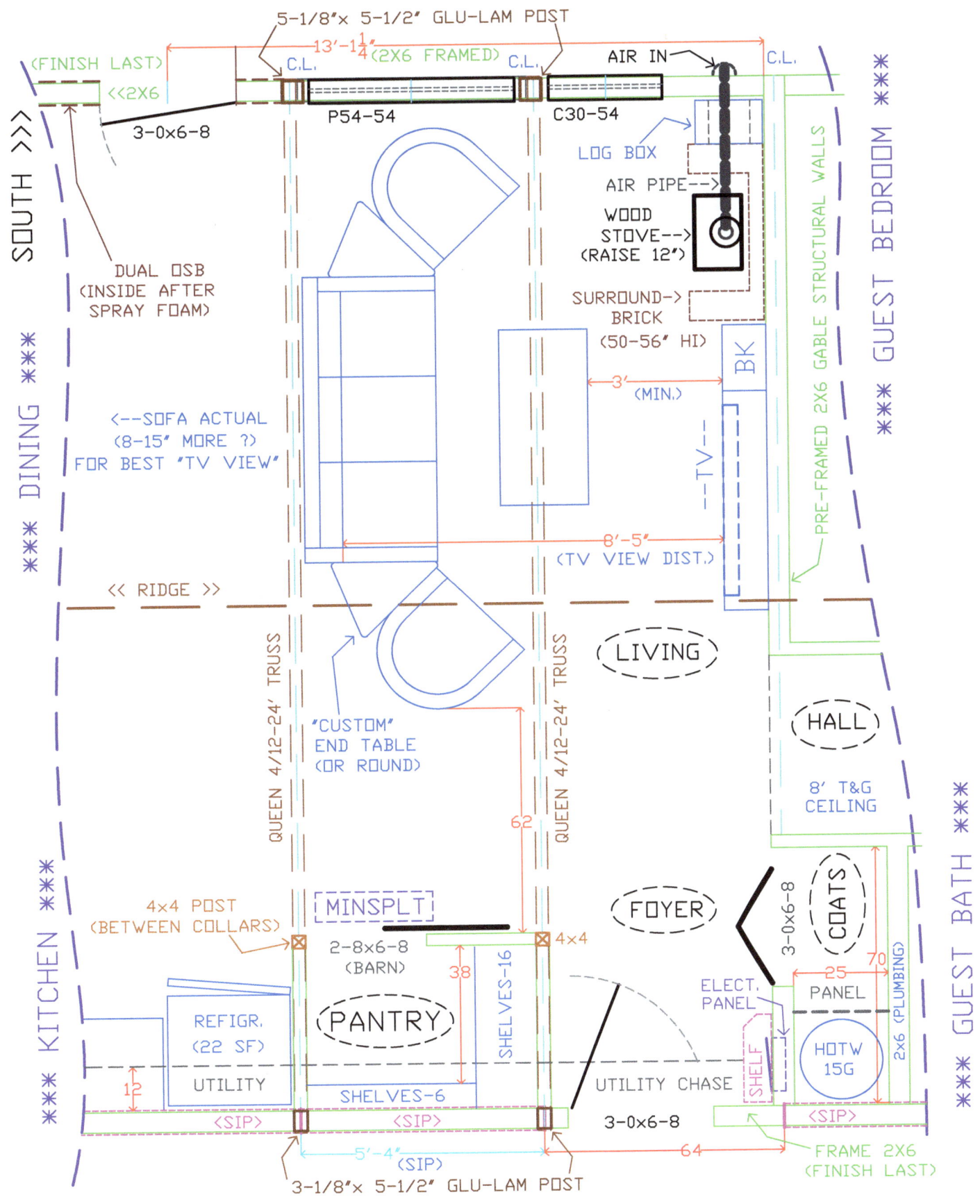

FIGURE 6.3 - "LIVING" ZONE DETAILS

GUEST BEDROOM ZONE

See Figure 6.4 opposite, page 40 >>>

GENERAL COMMENTS:

GUEST BEDROOM:

- _WINDOWS:_ two wider (36") casements (venting) on south wall
- Room for Queen bed, but aisle gaps, tighter (not intended for handicap access ***)
- Adequate closet for short-term guests

GUEST BATH:

- Slightly larger than, "apartment style layout", but not intended as full handicap rating ***
- A larger than standard size 30" x 60" tub, could fit here, with integrated shower wall style
    (note: need at least one bath _tub_ in home, many prefer shower only in Master bath)
- Sink vanity cabinet: suggest less deeper 18" (than typical 21") cabinet & 30" width
- Could consider wall-mount sink & toilet option for some handicap access improvement
- Linen cabinet; smaller, mounted above toilet
- Can adjust cabinet style/height, etc for some handicap improvement
- _Not_ elongated bowl style toilet, but do use _taller seat height_ version (about 18")
- Toilet position can shift some per preferred gap spacing (more near bath or to sink ?)

    * See Appendix 2 for notes on increasing home size for improved handicap rating**

CONSTRUCTION NOTES:

1. South window wall is 2x6 framed (best pre-made in shop, trailered to site, & then raised)
2. "Generic" (pre-made in shop) north & south versions of inner gable wall used here also
3. _North_ & _south_ gables built w/o door openings, etc., then cut & framed in _after erecting_
4. T&G _flat ceiling_ decking on truss collar tops & wall horizontal "nailers" = 104-1/2" height
5. Resulting loft zone above "Hall" aids utility routing and potential storage (access hatch?)
6. These short 2x4 internal walls can be field built or pre-made in shop also
7. Suggest spray foam the west bedroom wall shared with Living room (TV, sound?)

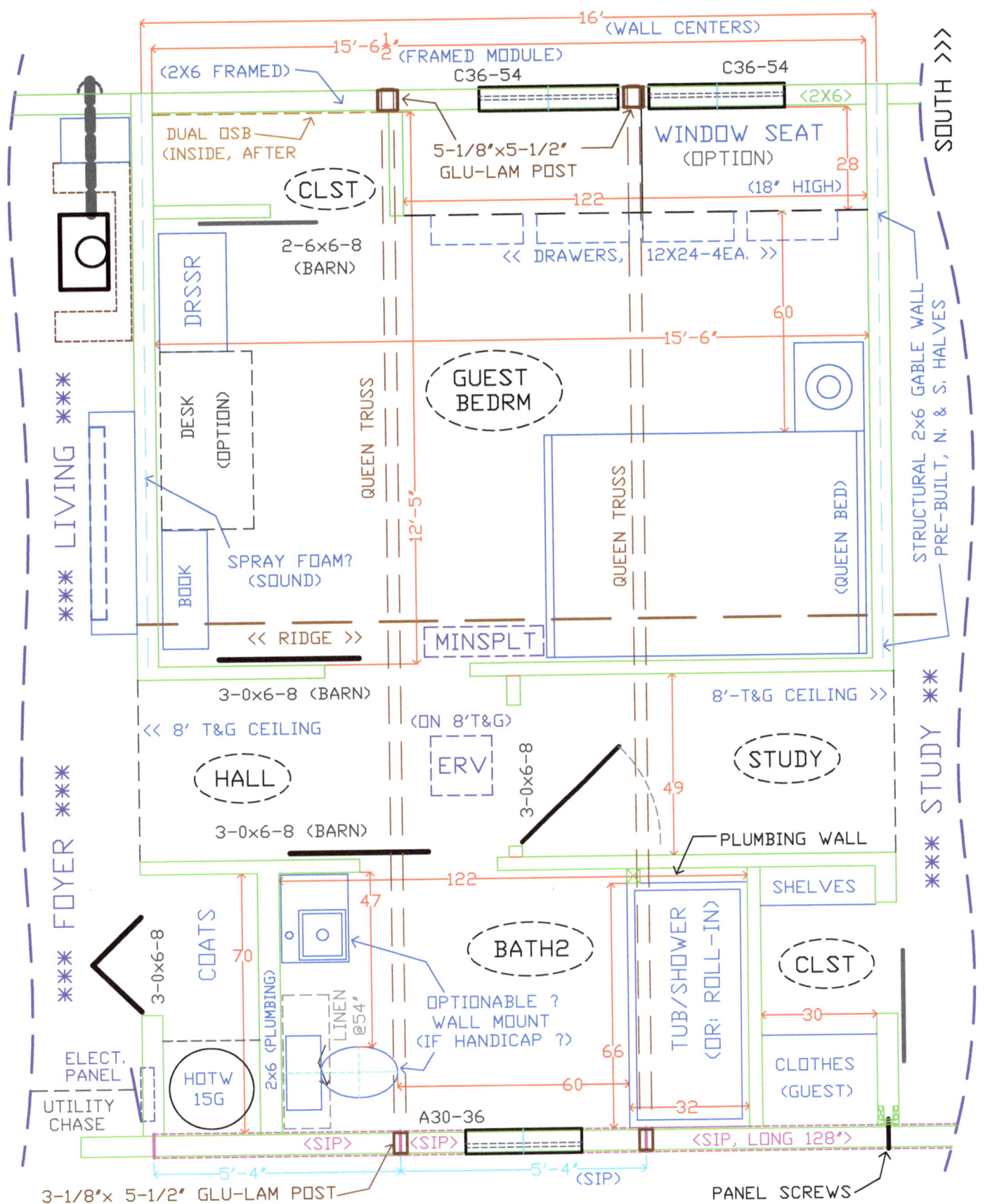

FIGURE 6.4 - "GUEST BEDROOM" ZONE DETAILS

STUDY ZONE

See Figure 6.5 opposite, page 42 >>>

GENERAL COMMENTS:

STUDY:

- <u>WINDOWS:</u> two wider (36"), 54" high, casements (venting) on south wall
- Extreme North & south ends of room = two "office nook" locations
- One wide, but low height, awning window (48"x36") on north wall (optimizes office nook)
- North file & bookcase = "low-boy" for printer spot & under 36" high north awning window
- Third, small (36" x 18") awning window on mid, high mount (about 80" top ?), west wall
- Futon/Bed on mid-west gable wall enables extra, temporary guest(s)
- Medium closet doubles as small guest hang-up clothes & office/study needs
- Longer southeast inner gable wall enables large or two small "Hobby" work tables
- Multiple bookcases (& depths & heights) adds to total storage space here
- Space for multiple size & height file cabinets (tall on SW end) for office functions

CONSTRUCTION NOTES:

1. West, high-mount awning window location decided early for SIP wall "shop drawings"
2. Mini-split (nearer to mid-east gable) utility bundle uses "loft" zone over hallway/bath
3. Hall doorway opening cut-in after erecting (added to shop pre-made 2x6 gables)
4. Electrical receptacle spots in SIP end gables = more than East house end? (for office needs?)
5. Framed south 2x6 wall aids access at Southwest corner for wire to SIP gable
6. Framed 2x6 east inner gable enables north wall SIP wiring run entry point
7. Possibly "minimal" quantity (code min, 12' max. gap?) electrical receptacles in SIP sections??
8. Upper gable "quadrants" (4/12 pitch trapezoid shape section) & center Glulam ridge post added later at framing erecting phase before Timber Trusses installed on wall
   > Absolutely critical that the framed Quadrants <u>match the Timber-Truss profile</u>
   > Frequently find that hand-framed versions inaccurate and also slow construction time
   > Best method is to build custom "JIG" as shown in **Simple Sip Homes** book (**> SSIP, C3, P50<**)

After the STUDY drawing, it is time to wrap up all this technical stuff . . .

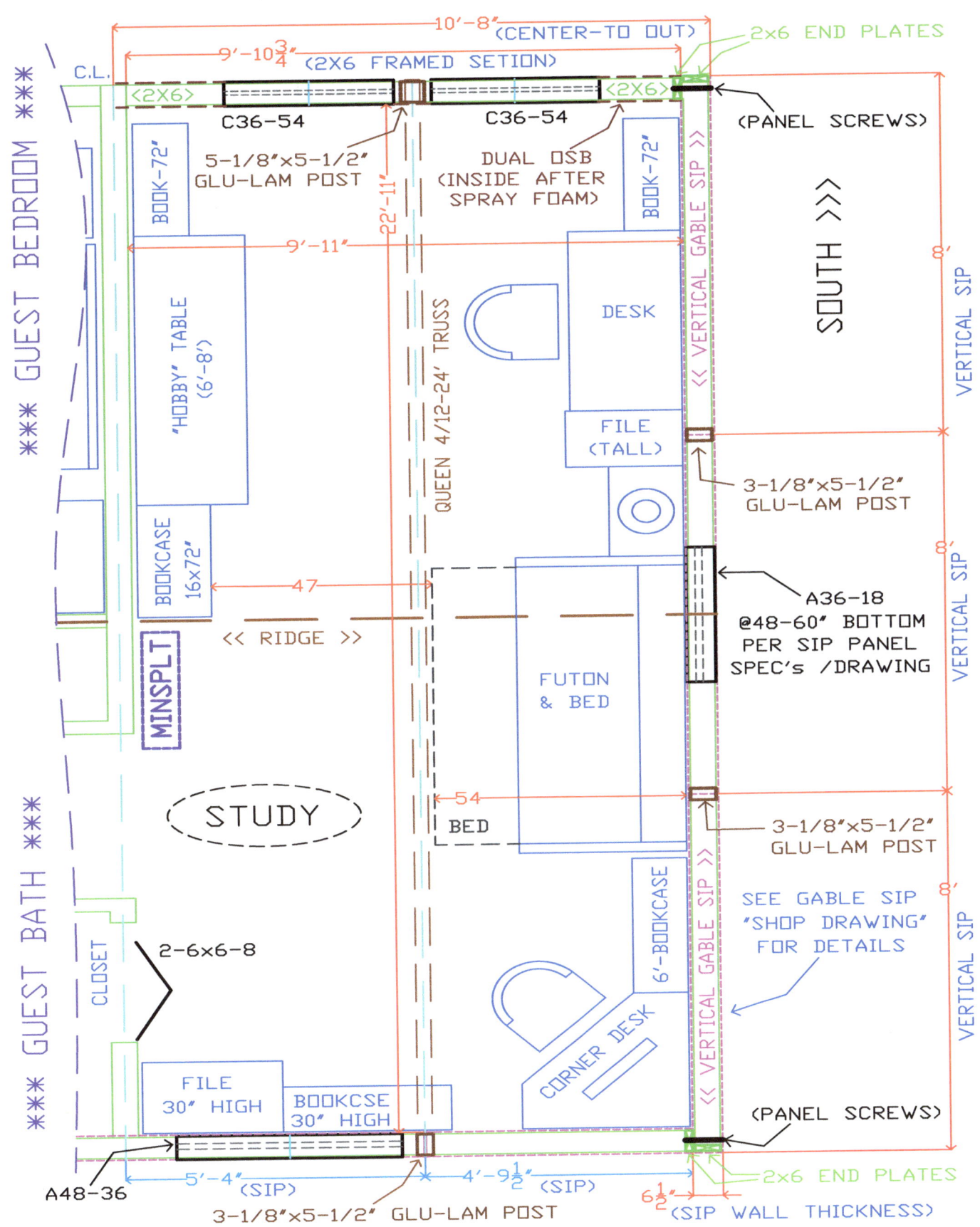

FIGURE 6.5 - "STUDY" ZONE DETAILS

CHAPTER 7 - WRAP UP

I trust, or at least hope, that the majority of readers now realize the importance of being more

"PRACTICAL"

for their retirement house choice. The focus on <u>real quality</u> structural details, principally on the home's <u>interior</u>, and less emphasis on the exterior appearance, or "curb appeal" features will produce a <u>more comfortable</u>, trouble-free, later-in-life, abode.

The technical points presented here should influence our readers in their planning process for that key life-phase goal. One last, but very significant, and yet not often discussed, residential construction industry reference point should also be factored into this decision process:

TYPICAL BUILT (or "To Code") HOUSES:

- *The vast majority of homes built in the US are only to the standard "building codes"*
- *Those building codes are just a **"minimum"** requirement*

- *Which kind of means just "barely passing" . . .*
- *OR : many of those homes could be thought of as just a **"D+"** rating*

So, in parting here, I am challenging the readers:

<u>What type of home do you want to live in during your retirement years</u>

? ? ?

Our choice is very much like this :

(Nephew DJ's very similar home's south elevation)　　　　　*(photo by DJ)*

APPENDIX 1 – REFERENCES

1- *Simple S.I.P. Homes* , by Art Smith,

ISBN: 978-0-578-69700-0, Aug. 2020

2- *BUILDING TODAY's GREEN HOME* , by Art Smith,

ISBN: 978-1-55870-862-4, Aug. 2009

3- *Structural Insulated Panels (SIPS)* , by Michael Morley

ISBN: 1-56158-351-0, 2000

4- *THE PASSIVE SOLAR ENERGY BOOK* , by Edward Mazria

ISBN: 0-87857-237-6, 1979

5- *HARDIE ® is registered to JAMES HARDIE Co.*

6- *Ice & Watershield ® is registered to W.R. Grace & Co.*

7- *MARATHON ® is registered to RHEEM MANUFACTURING COMPANY*

8- *TimberLOK ®, HeadLOK ®, & LedgerLOK ® are registerd to FastenMaster, by Olympic*

9- *ZAC ® is registered to SFS USA*

APPENDIX 2 – HANDICAP HOUSE EXPANSION NOTES

If the homeowner really needs a more-handicap friendly home, the realistic option is to increase the home size. For example, adding one more Timber truss zone (64") in the Guest bedroom zone. Some text suggestions below (no drawings provided here) should provide some guidance on this issue.

1. Add additional Timber Truss to guest room with the resulting 64" increase in house length (now 69'-4" long, and total area = 1664 s.f.)

2. Guest bedroom now can copy the triple window scheme as in the master bedroom

3. Closet area shifts to west wall (shared with living room), rotated 90 degrees and about 5 ft long now with dual 30" bi-fold doors?

4. Entry door shifts east, increase hall length about 29"

5. Study closet on west end of increased bathroom potential area (using about 29" of the 64" bathroom increase)

6. The 35" net increase in the Bath2 room length is allocated to more spacing around the tub, toilet, sink vanity, & linen cabinet new sizing

APPENDIX 3 – READER REQUESTING MORE INFORMATION

The author would like to provide more technical information, even some drawings, etc. on a very limited basis. But due to potential liability for construction work in distant locations with unknown local code specifics, and construction by unknown skilled contractors, a "Liability Waiver" for the author of some sort will be needed. *** Also, a "positive" interface with prospective homeowner is very important to the author to even begin discussions.

SUGGESTED PROCEDURE FOR OBTAINING MORE INFORMATION

1- *Locate the authors book review website: www.simplesiphomes.com*

2- *Find the author's current email on the top right of screen*

3- *Send the author a polite, brief, but decent overview of your project, location, budget, general goals, construction work timing, homeowner's building experience, and if a general contractor is involved (GC & your constuction experience).*

4- *Pending review, author will try to respond in a reasonable time period (1-2 weeks, retired, but busy!)*

*** Drawings are intended for North Georgia county zoning & building codes and example of what the author would build here. The homeowner has to be responsible to verify that these plans would pass their own local codes. In fact, they should have a local P.E. (Professional Engineer) verify. For example, extreme northern zones will require more snow load on the roof Timber Trusses. Thus, the homeowner may need to increase the truss bolt grades to 5 in general and even 8 at the two end collars points. Plus, a higher grade Glu-Lam rafter beam may be required (from the standard FB =2400#, to a premium level at some glulam vendors (like Anthony's Power-Beam, higher 3600# FB bending rating.)